SINK OR SHINE

SINK OR SHINE

ATTRACT CLIENTS AND TALENT WITH THE BRIGHTNESS OF YOUR MISSION

ADAM H. MICHAELS

WITH DAYNA WILLIAMS

LIONCREST
PUBLISHING

SINK OR SHINE

Attract Clients and Talent with the Brightness of Your Mission

ISBN   978-1-5445-0228-1 *Paperback*
       978-1-5445-0229-8 *Ebook*

This book is dedicated to my loving and tolerant wife Jodi and our beautiful children Lilah and Dylan. They and those like them are the unsung heroes behind every successful entrepreneur, supporting us even in our craziest and most irrational moments. I love you more!

CONTENTS

TARGET AUDIENCE

May this book serve as both a timely inspiration and an electric jolt to:

- **Entrepreneurs**—who are just starting out or who are in the early stages of establishing a business—may you heed these words of advice, and build an exceptional organization that defines your marketplace to attract clients and talent with the brightness of your mission.
- **Wanta-preneurs**—who are on a journey toward entrepreneurism, but currently lack the idea, knowledge, or capital to do so today—may this book keep you from making unnecessary mistakes along the way.
- **Intrapreneurs**—those that seek to utilize their entrepreneurial disposition inside a company—may you search and find an organization that will provide rich

experiences, investing in you so that you can amass the knowledge and expertise to fulfill your purpose.

- **Business leaders of mid-sized to large-sized organizations**—may you reexamine the status quo, challenge your assumptions, and embrace the possibilities of throwing out the old playbook in an effort to redefine yourself for prolific growth.

- **Employees working within companies**—may you secure the stability you sought when you chose a "job" over self-employment by realizing the power, potential, and responsibility of your individual influence to become the remarkable leader and indispensable contributor you were born to be.

INTRODUCTION

THE BIG IDEA

The promise of America as the land of opportunity, as established and modeled by our forefathers, has stalled out for many. Obtaining the American Dream through the Horacio Alger ideal of bootstrapping your way up the class ladder has given way to widespread cynicism, with a large portion of the population looking for answers.

Modern class stagnation and economic immobility have been compounded by example after example of bad behavior by institutions that were once revered by the American public. For their part, businesses aren't exempt from this phenomenon, and, in fact, they have become a big part of the problem. Decades of greed, broken promises, and self-centeredness have significantly eroded consumer and employee confidence.

Growing tension because of inequality due to race, gender, sexual orientation, and social class is boiling over and putting at risk the future viability of an America that Ronald Reagan envisioned as a "shining city upon a hill whose beacon light guides freedom-loving people everywhere."

Rather than waiting for politicians to set aside their agendas and special interests or for schools to actually educate our children and young adults, we have another, far superior option. I have long believed that capitalism, and moreover **entrepreneurism**, is the answer to many of the ills that plague our society. Turning toward entrepreneurism has the full potential to obliterate economic immobility. Entrepreneurism creates jobs. It raises the standard of living—and not just for these enterprising individuals themselves, but for all Americans. Ultimately, entrepreneurism delivers socialist ends through capitalist means, allowing people to be their best, to pursue their passions, and to contribute to the world as God intended.

The real power of entrepreneurism is that it doesn't discriminate against anyone based on social class. It ignores whether you are black, white, Native American, Hispanic, Asian, Pacific Islander, or "other," and it doesn't care whether you are male, female, trans, non-binary, gay, straight, or something else entirely. It has no preference whether you are Christian, Jewish, Muslim, or atheist. And, it doesn't give a damn about what college you went to or if you didn't go to college at all. Entrepreneurism is not subjective. It takes grit and rewards talent, effort, and execution indiscriminately, leaving no room for income inequality or glass ceilings.

Sink or Shine is about taking a hard look at some deeply held modern beliefs. It's about confronting the stubborn, self-defeating behavior that keeps organizations from thriving and constrains our personal effectiveness, leaders, and contributors. American capitalism has the power to transform communities, families, and individuals. Together, we can re-establish America as the grand lighthouse that will lead the way in ushering in a new era of prosperity and American exceptionalism.

AN INSTINCT FOR HUSTLE

I've been selling things for as long as I can remember. Early on, I got addicted to the "thrill of the kill." The money wasn't bad either, but the thrill was unlike anything I'd ever experienced.

My infatuation with the adrenaline rush of someone handing me a stack of money led my nine-year-old self to set up shop outside of my mother's workplace—American Press in Neptune, New Jersey. I sold off-cuts of paper as pads and split the profits with Bud, the owner. Even at that age, I was unrelenting in my drive for sales. Every passerby was a new opportunity to hone my pitch, and all but a few left with an armful of goods they didn't know they wanted until they crossed my path.

While I didn't quite have the same level of ingenuity as the Girl Scout who sold her cookies outside of a marijuana dispensary, I still charmed my way to a rather impressive $127 in just a few short hours. Other businesses followed. I started a snow-removal service, signing my neighbors up for annual snow-removal contracts—my earliest foray into insurance. I formed a golf-ball reclamation and restoration business where I would sneak onto the golf course after-hours and wade through the water traps to collect lost balls. After cleaning, polishing, and sorting them by brand, I sold them back to golfers at a price of four balls for a dollar.

Armed with a basic understanding of supply and demand, I built a candy empire from the back of the school bus, thanks in part to an uncle who worked at Topps Candy Company and gifted me a treasure trove of Bazooka bubblegum. I fortified my supply with later trips to Price Club—the predecessor of Costco and Sam's Club. I bought sweets in bulk until I got busted for dealing Pixy Stix in the third grade.

I was always "that kid." I was the kid with the hustle, the kid with the plan. If you're reading this, it's likely you were "that kid" too.

It wasn't until I studied economics in high school that I became interested in the business of business. My teacher at the time was Marty Lefsky, a man with a wardrobe straight from the 1970s and hair sculpted into a helmet that would make Darth Vader jealous. Mr. Lefsky revealed that the "high" of the sale was only part of the story.

Through Keynes, Locke, and Friedman, I learned about the forces of capitalism and Adam Smith's "Invisible Hand." I delved deeper into the concepts of supply and demand, of scarcity and opportunity. I discovered that the definition of entrepreneurism was having the ability to recognize opportunities and organize production, and having a willingness to accept risk in pursuit and attainment of a reward. These teachings led to an epiphany.

Though I liked sports, I wasn't a jock. I got good grades, but I wasn't a nerd. I smoked pot and loved live music, but I wasn't a burner. I loved early techno, but I wasn't a raver. *I was an entrepreneur.*

This realization put my adolescent identity crisis behind me and allowed me to adjust my focus. By the time I arrived at The George Washington University on an academic scholarship, I was already plotting my next business venture.

Washington, DC was filled with opportunities for students from the local universities to test out the quality of their fake IDs and spend their parents' money, so I zeroed in on nightclub promotion as my business of choice. My partner, Aaron Sanor, and I negotiated deals with local bars and nightclubs and delved into insurance a second time by accepting the risk associated with guaranteeing a certain level of bar receipts in exchange for the proceeds collected at the door. We hired and managed a team of sales reps who hit the streets with palm cards and flyers to promote our events. We also hired bouncers to provide security and collect cover charges at the front door.

Venues filled, profits soared, and I learned a host of valuable skills firsthand: planning, marketing, advertising, negotiation, risk management, and human resources. I was also en route to a 3.0—but unfortunately, it was my blood alcohol level and not my GPA.

It is probably as cliché for entrepreneurs to have a distaste for formal education as it is for strippers to have daddy issues. My frustration with academia stemmed from a combination of the monotony of classes I knew would have zero relevance to my future and an itching compulsion to take action, to go after whatever was next. It was clear to me that my real-world experience was going to be more valuable than classroom theory. Besides, I wasn't intellectually stimulated by my biology or calculus classes. There were times I considered dropping out altogether. Instead, I pursued an internship at Smith Barney and then proceeded to convince the gentleman for whom I worked to sponsor me for my Series-7 license. By the time I was nineteen, I was a stockbroker and traded in my club gear for a suit and tie.

It didn't take me long to begin appreciating success, all the while hearing questions from friends like, "Why are you wasting the best years of your life?" I was confident that this was the road I was meant to take. I was hustling during one of the biggest bull markets in history. I quickly realized that, though I was good at telling stories, the work was rather unfulfilling. I secured client monies and our managers turned little piles of money into bigger piles of money (most of the time). It seemed that no matter how well I did, they were unsatisfied, always wanting more.

Still, despite my age and inexperience, my hustle opened doors. David Morningstar, the same gentleman who gave me a chance as an intern, invited me to join him in starting The Executive Management Group. EMG was going to be a different kind of financial services firm. Rather than selling to mom and pop across the dinner table, we would sell across the boardroom table. We focused on issues that impacted businesses and the employees that worked for them. Rather than telling emotional stories that moved people off the schneid to buy stocks and bonds, we solved problems that plagued entrepreneurs and kept them from reaching their full potential. We helped them contain costs, increase profits, reduce taxes, and improve employee loyalty.

One of the products in our arsenal, through a company called the American Family Life Assurance Company of Columbus, allowed us to solve challenges that had arisen as a direct result of the shifting of costs from employers to employees. Through employee-funded, tax-favored benefit enhancements and bringing companies into federal compliance, we made our clients more profitable and enhanced employee benefits in the process at zero cost. It was one of the rare scenarios where something that sounds almost too good to be true actually was.

By the time the company went through a brand overhaul and launched its advertising campaign with the now iconic duck, David and I had decided to pivot and turn EMG into a full-blown Aflac agency. In 2002, after finishing at one of the top operations in the company, I left the Baltimore–Washington area to start anew, pioneering an undeveloped Chicago market. Over the next seven years, we were tested and responded by building a model for urban growth scaling to five offices, more than 250 associates, and more than 2,500 B2B clients. In 2009, I sought yet another challenge. This time, it wasn't building from scratch but rather taking over for a legend who was beloved by his team—Joe Buzzello. In the subsequent seven years, we doubled from $16 to $32 million in annual sales, outpacing much of the company.

In 2015, I launched a web series on Elevate with Adam, in conjunction with taking on a corporate role as Vice President of the West Territory, where I was responsible for a team that consisted of nearly 5,000 individuals who collectively produced more than $256 million in sales to more than 72,000 B2B clients and their employees.

Elevate with Adam was intended to socialize my leadership and sales philosophies, along with providing entrepreneurial insight to the intrapreneurs within my organization, to recreate the intimate connection that had served me so well in the past. In short order, it became apparent that my message was resonating with my team and impacting the culture and results in a positive way, as we quickly became the top performing operation in the nation. What was unexpected was the engagement with so many people outside of my ecosystem—those not on my team. Perhaps all it took was Jay-Z's proclamation, "I'm not a businessman, I'm a business, (pregnant pause) man!" for the American Dream to seem more accessible to those who previously felt marginalized. These entrepreneurs, wanta-preneurs, and those inside of traditional organizations were sharing and liking my posts and commenting that "it was exactly what they needed to hear." The positive response invigorated and inspired me to do more. I knew that identifying the path to the American Dream was only the first step, and I knew I had more I could share.

This sentiment is a big part of why I endeavored to write this book. It is also why I reached out to my co-writer, Dayna Williams, to solicit her help and perspective. She and I have known each other for several years. As soon as I met her, I immediately recognized her as a genuine talent. Dayna was on a team of consultants Aflac had hired to address numerous issues they were facing on a broad scale with conversion, retention, and coaching. As we began swapping ideas and experiences, I immediately recognized the synergies between our shared viewpoints—particularly around radical candor. Dayna has been an unbelievable thought partner, instrumental in helping to further define the provocative concepts in this book and build a roadmap for practical execution. While I've spent years on the inside building and leading organizations, Dayna has spent the last eighteen-plus years of her career as a talent development consultant on the outside, looking in. She brings a wealth of perspective and has shared with me countless stories and examples of failure and dysfunction, considering just how much time and money is spent on hiring experts, and how quickly that expertise is diluted or abandoned. As a result, businesses are left with the same gaps, challenges, and issues that led them to reach out and seek expertise in the first place. Together, Dayna and I marvel at this failure and wonder how long it will be before some of the most recognizable businesses of today will be replaced because of their inability to change.

This book is a compilation of our perspectives. It comes from more than forty years of combined interactions with thousands of businesses. It is the byproduct of actions taken, actions ignored, and lessons learned the hard way. It is a look through the many lenses of entrepreneurs, intrapreneurs, consultants, and corporate insiders. We believe that those who read it cover to cover will walk away with "exactly what they needed to hear."

TUGBOATS & LIGHTHOUSES

In the following chapters, we'll make the case that there are two types of businesses: **Tugboats** and **Lighthouses.** The Tugboats represent the antiquated ways of the past. Their barnacled bottoms and rust-covered exteriors show the wear and tear of their workhorse ways. Their tired appearance is a telltale sign of their imminent decline, despite their historical effectiveness. Though they may have dominated in their day, their underlying structural damage places them in jeopardy of being sunk by the realities of the modern marketplace.

Conversely, the majestic Lighthouse is a thing of timeless beauty whose "guiding light" is the great differentiator. Not only does the Lighthouse serve as a defining landmark on the shoreline, but it becomes a destination for all who are searching for it and some who happen upon it by mistake. Grounded in their mission through a solid foundation, Lighthouses are built to last—impervious to unyielding environmental changes.

The fact is that most established businesses and the leaders within them are romantic about the successes of the past. They operate like Tugboats, refusing to venture beyond the break walls of the harbors they know so well. They seek comfort and what they believe is the guarantee of safe passage, unaware that their vessels are eroding. This commitment to the status quo and slowness to adapt will sadly become the epitaph inscribed upon the memory of what they will claim was "the perfect storm," in spite of fair warning.

To that end, this book is an unapologetic, direct conversation about what it takes to thrive in today's environment. We will take a deep look into what has changed in the engagement of consumers and employees alike. We will then shift our focus to the power, importance, and potential of being mission-driven before dissecting the many elements associated with talent, culture, and leadership. By the end, we will shine the light on the importance of amplifying your mission to the marketplace.

Of course, all this discussion is for naught if it isn't combined with application and action—so along the way, you'll have opportunities to reflect and, in the end, you'll have created a blueprint to follow as you build a remarkable Lighthouse of your own.

PART 1

SEA OF CHANGE

CHAPTER 1

A QUICK AND DIRTY HISTORY

There was a time when businesses and their surrogates were trusted members of society. A time when employees sought to find a career that offered the permanent stability of a corporate ladder to climb and a suitable pension. It was also a time when society saw businesses as iconic parts of the American tapestry. The faces of those businesses belonged to our neighbors, fellow parishioners at our places of worship, and pillars within our local communities. Businesses were earnest in their goals and honorable in their actions to garner the trust and adoration of the community at large.

Throughout American history, the relationship between businesses and "the people" has been a prominent force in solidifying our nation's place in the global society. At times, such as during and after World War I and II, consumerism was considered a patriotic duty among even the most frugal, in support of the war effort. Buying "Made in America" goods was a point of national pride.

Yet, as the global economy has exploded, spending is no longer widely viewed as a patriotic act; consumerism has become little more than a way to fulfill our desire for stuff. You'd think that selling goods and products in this landscape of rabid consumerism would be easier than it was in the past, but it's not. Somewhere after the end of the Industrial Revolution and after Madonna declared that "we are living in a material world," everything changed.

WHAT HAPPENED?

Before dead-bolting our doors and pretending not to be home became culturally acceptable, door-to-door sales transactions were common. Salesmen peddled everything from vacuums to cosmetics. They leveraged the inherent politeness of homemakers who welcomed them and their trademark sample cases into their kitchens to offer their pitch while downing a glass of homemade lemonade. Not long after these homemakers left for burgeoning careers in the workforce, telemarketing became more efficient and more prominent.

Most people over the age of forty-five remember the dread and annoyance of these calls that relentlessly interrupted every meal you sat down for. This was particularly the case before the advent of caller ID. After answering the phone, you would hear the token two-second delay followed by something that started out like, "Mrs. Everly? Hi, this is Bill from New Success Enterprises. I have been authorized to offer you a one-time..." and you would summarily hang up before they could finish. Eventually, you stopped answering altogether—and today, most people don't even have a landline.

Next came email. At first, the three little words "you've got mail" would send people straight to the computer, excited to read the new message, regardless of whether the sender was a former love interest, a progressive business entity offering discounts, newsletters, or maybe even the opportunity of a lifetime. But it wasn't long before targeted strategies turned into shotgun spam campaigns with no strategic merit. Consumers again disengaged by hitting delete.

THE SHIFT OF POWER

The barrage of indiscriminately sent messages from marketers and would-be employers has left people feeling inundated and disenchanted. Rather than achieving higher conversion rates and runaway results, businesses have been left scratching their heads wondering what else they can do. To many businesses, consumers look fickle and unreliable when it's hard to entice them. And it isn't just sales. Employee recruitment is increasingly challenging, too, and hiring and recruiting costs have increased dramatically. It's almost as if no one—neither potential customers nor potential employees—has much interest in hearing from or being involved with these companies.

Big businesses can look out of touch, if not downright manipulative. The growing distaste for everything associated with big businesses isn't only prevalent among those who are Anonymous or Occupying Wall Street. This dissatisfaction and distrust bridges the spectrum of political ideologies, and the common denominator is the sheer wealth of information available to people looking to make informed decisions. Today's consumers and candidates are more informed than at any other time in history. As such, they have high expectations for transparency and a low tolerance for "the game," which is really nothing more than the abuse of power that has resided in the hands of businesses for the better part of the last century. Consumer reports and customer reviews mean potential buyers don't just rely on a company's own sales pitch. Meanwhile, online search engines and websites like Glassdoor, Indeed, and LinkedIn provide job seekers with copious amounts of information, and that gives them the upper hand in the search for value.

Thanks in part to changing priorities and an increased desire to control one's own destiny, consumers and job candidates have taken back control faster than they can say "Alexa," "Siri," or "Google."

THE PERIL OF STATUS QUO

Out of touch leaders and those who are appreciating success in leadership roles or a part of a strong business effort may think, "But we are killing it right now! We have an incredible team in place and more business than we can handle." It is easy to become intoxicated by one's success. Of course, any boss would brag about the bonuses they just paid out and remark about the research they did to ensure their employees' total compensation was in line with or better than the industry standard. They'd mention the high-fives in the break room and the high morale after bonuses, the cutting-edge, best-in-class tools they're using to grow revenue while creating efficiencies that bolster the bottom line. And without question, those sales and marketing teams would use the latest buzz words to talk about how they're leveraging SEO, retargeting, and experimenting with the early stages of Artificial Intelligence (AI), machine learning, and all manner of emerging, experiential programs. I would smile while I listened, and I'd have to shake that business leader's hand. They should be commended for all of it.

But the fact is that without these things, the business you operate as an owner or entrepreneur, lead as an executive, or contribute to as an intrapreneur or employee would not have survived up until now—just ask the folks at Toys"R"Us or Kodak. Even this kind of good, thoughtful leadership doesn't count as innovation when it's the basic common denominator necessary to a business's survival in the current marketplace. Regardless of the role you play, this book is designed to challenge you to look squarely into the future. It is about DNA-level changes to forge unwavering sustainability in the face of a sea of change. A sea in which Deloitte estimates that 66 percent of all of a business's current employees are statistically either actively or passively considering a career change.[1] It is likewise a business environment where 52 percent of all of the companies that were listed on Fortune 500 in the year 2000 are no longer on the list.[2] Shocking as this may seem, it is more compelling to consider that there will likely be a 100 percent turnover by 2077.

Our intention is not to be alarmist—though, honestly, we're kind of alarmed. We simply mean to point out that either things will change or things will change. Your busi-

---

1   "Talent Edge 2020: Building the Recovery Together." Deloitte United States. Accessed December 21, 2018. https://www2.deloitte.com/insights/us/en/topics/talent/talent-edge-2020-building-the-recovery-together.html.

2   "Digital Transformation Is Racing Ahead and No Industry Is." Harvard Business Review. March 09, 2018. Accessed December 21, 2018. https://hbr.org/sponsored/2017/07/digital-transformation-is-racing-ahead-and-no-industry-is-immune-2.

ness will either be a victor in this environment because of your ability to adjust your strategy, or you will be a casualty of inaction. My good friend Paul Kovensky is CEO of the Kove Collection. A restaurateur and hotelier with eighteen properties, he's a great example of a flourishing business leader, and he maintains a generous and forward-looking perspective. He's always quick to declare "there is always room at the top." Our hope is that you will begin to see the world the way people experiencing unbridled success do.

CHAPTER 2

THE REFLEXIVE NO

It's 7:27 a.m. on a typical, middle-of-the-week workday. You haven't even finished your first cup of coffee to help you regain consciousness yet, and Michael Strahan interrupts the morning news during a commercial break to declare that Metamucil is "one small change that can lead to good things." You quickly dismiss it, knowing that your cup of Joe will be all you need to *get going*.

You don't care about whatever commercial is to follow, so you look down at your smartphone only to realize that your inbox doubled in size overnight with offers from Canadian drug companies offering "cheaper," "bigger," and "longer." You unceremoniously delete them knowing that if you have a change of heart (or even if you don't), they will reappear tomorrow.

You get into your car, and before you can even pull out of the driveway, the morning DJ launches into a poorly written monologue about his "favorite" car company that just so happens to sponsor the show. Unconvinced and unimpressed, you switch to Sirius Satellite for some interruption-free music—a service you're immediately reminded is worth every penny.

As you drive out of your neighborhood and onto the main highway, roadside billboards bombard you immediately, enticing you to take a detour to satiate your hunger pangs. One lets you know your Egg McMuffin is only two miles ahead. Another implores you to "EAT MOR CHIKIN." You consider stopping until you recall this morning's Facebook-generated "memory" reminding you that a few years ago, you didn't have a double chin. You drive on.

Eventually, you get to work. Before tackling your to-do list, you take a moment to check last night's sports scores in the hopes of finding the news of another glorious New York Rangers victory and, more than likely, New York Knicks defeat. This information is held hostage by a pre-roll ad for an indistinguishable razor company. You ignore it and focus squarely on the countdown in the bottom right corner. *Five...four...*you begin vigorously left clicking...*three...two...one...*SKIP!

Throughout the day, you're interrupted by auto-dialers

offering guaranteed business loans and targeted ads suggesting it's time to purchase the television you've been religiously researching on CNET and TechRadar to buy before this weekend's big game. You ignore the suggestion to "Click Now" to impulse-buy the TV, because you have a plan to stop at a big box store on your way home this evening.

As you enter the store with the financial means and honest-to-goodness intention of making a purchase—it happens. The continuous marketing assault and badgering of the day is made manifest the moment the salesperson in the blue shirt with the bright yellow logo approaches with a friendly, "Can I help you?"

In an effort to avoid a sales pitch, you avoid eye contact, and immediately your Reflexive No presents itself in the form of an outright lie: "No, I'm just looking." You refuse to relinquish control and beeline for the TV section.

Emboldened by your assertion of self-determination, you survey the wall of TVs looking for the one with the highest quality picture for the lowest cost. When you've narrowed it down to three, you find yourself straining to read the small print on the index cards. All are 65" 4K Ultra HD TVs. The LG is $799. The Samsung is $1,399, and the Sony is $1,499. The picture quality seems relatively similar, so you can't figure out why the prices are so significantly different. You pride yourself on being rational with a willingness to pay a premium for quality, but you want to understand the differences and get a good deal. Silently, you stand lost in a sea of comparison. You stretch your neck and loudly clear your throat in hopes to get the attention of the expert you summarily dismissed moments earlier—to no avail. Your hope for expert help quickly degenerates into irritation about poor customer service. Rather than wait any longer, you think, *"F*&k it, I have Amazon Prime,"* and abandon your plan, leaving the store empty-handed. You retreat to the comfort of your own home, where you take the intel you collected at the store and cross-reference it with the star ratings and comments offered by random strangers to come to your conclusion. You justify your buying modality—trading personal service for convenience—thinking, "at least I don't have to schlep it home," since your new television will be delivered to your doorstep before 10:00 a.m. the next day.

THE RISE OF THE REFLEXIVE NO

If only that example were an isolated incident. In reality, this scenario plays itself out over and over again whether a consumer is buying coffee or a car. Years of noise, shady advertising, and unsavory sales practices have resulted in a phenomenon we call the **Reflexive No**. The Reflexive No is born out of the human desire to reclaim control in an environment where capitalism may appear to be running amuck. In a sense, the Reflexive No is an internal bullshit screen; its acuity is fine-tuned through the sum total of all of life's experiences. It is the instinct that is triggered when a potential buyer identifies the inauthenticity of a canned sales pitch. It is the nauseated feeling that overcomes us when we're drowning in thousands of poorly written emails suggesting "perceived synergies," or when a crusty salesman deploys the outdated and overused Tom Hopkins classic, "I understand how you *feel*, Roger. In fact, most of my clients *felt* exactly the same way, but what I have *found*..." Blech!

For decades, businesses' bad behavior and outright abuse of the consumer have compounded over and over again. The consequence for this flagrancy is that consumers are completely shut down to even the most well-rehearsed sales approach. The people they are trying to reach have effectively iced them out and will only engage if and when they are ready, and they will do so strictly on their terms. Multimillion-dollar advertising and promotional budgets simply don't have the return on investment they once did. This is devastating to businesses. Without an evolution of practices and a reimagination of their entire strategy, the average business is bound to find it increasingly difficult to survive.

Consumers have become their own best gatekeepers and

arbiters of what works for them and when. These savvy shoppers are aware of the "tricks of the trade" and can spot them faster than love notes from a Nigerian Prince. A perfect illustration comes from the infamous car industry, known for its canned sales pitches and shady practices. Describing someone as a "used car salesman" is the ultimate insult, conjuring up a visceral image of someone scummy, slimy, and deceitful. Even those used car salesmen who are honest are still held in contempt for the past damage done by their peer group.

There was a time in the past when a car salesman would ask, "What do I have to do to get you to take this car home today?" and get an honest and forthright answer from an unwitting consumer. Likewise, when that same deceitful salesperson falsely attempted to create urgency by claiming, "This is the fastest-selling car on the lot!" some unsuspecting buyers rushed to make a move out of a fear of missing out. But those days are behind us (or at least quickly coming to an end).

Studies show that the average car buyer visits thirteen or more websites to gather information before making a purchase. Undoubtedly, they come across at least one site that exalts techniques to avoid being scammed, explaining the intricacies of the "Ben Franklin Close," the "I have to talk to the General Manager" schtick, the "Savior Strategy," or the "Four-Square Method." So, when salespeople try these techniques, the informed consumer's guard immediately goes up and disengagement ensues.

Twenty-five years ago, consumer frustration led to the meteoric rise of CarMax, who pioneered the concept of "no-haggle pricing" specifically to head this traditional car-shopping headache off at the pass. CarMax's choice to acknowledge and respond directly to this common consumer concern changed the car buying and selling landscape. Still, it was widespread access to the internet that really leveled the playing field through increased transparency and evolved strategies. Tesla, a different kind of car manufacturer, has forgone the dealership model altogether, opting instead for showrooms in upscale shopping malls where buyers appreciate a bespoke buying experience. They select their own options and craft their cars from the wheels up. Companies such as TrueCar, Carvana, Shift, and Fair let people purchase new and used cars from an app on a smartphone. This is not only convenient, it offers car shoppers the ability to avoid the painful dealership sales charade. This is also precisely the reason I buy my cars exclusively through my auto broker—Arlen at Vici Auto Group, who leverages his expertise to negotiate the best deal possible by pitting dealers against one another. The value he adds results in a no-hassle experience that includes everything from soup to nuts until my new car arrives on my doorstep.

Despite the energy and shrewdness it takes to navigate

all of the lame sales tactics, market misinformation, and overall noise, the fact is that when consumers are ready to buy, they are often better informed than they've been at any point in history. Modern consumers want candor, honesty, and price transparency. This new reality forces businesses that want to thrive to aggressively confront the status quo when it comes to their overall strategy.

BOTTOM LINE

Consumers are so inundated with sales and advertising messaging that they experience a visceral negative response to nearly anything that feels "salesy." The noise that consumes our waking hours has led to fatigue, irritation, and numbing of attention. No one wants to be sold to, and that has morphed into a perpetually defensive posture. This consumer disengagement is the consequence of years of bad behavior by businesses and sales professionals who not only inundated the marketplace but also overpromised and repeatedly underdelivered. Dealing with this attitudinal shift is critical for businesses and employers alike. While it represents a barrier for those still embracing the old model of transacting with consumers, it provides an opportunity for those willing to meet customers where they are.

REFLECT

1. Consider your personal attitudes around how you make purchasing decisions. When do you prefer the do-it-yourself method, and when would you rather enlist the help of a sales professional?

2. If you spend time researching before a purchase, what factors are most important to you and why?

3. Now consider your own customers and employees. What are you doing to capture their attention and imagination?

4. If potential customers (or employees) are searching for your product of service (or career opportunities), will they find you?

CHAPTER 3

GREAT EXPECTATIONS

It's not just consumers whose behavior is changing. Employees are engaging differently as well. Throughout most of the twentieth century, employment and unemployment were predicated mostly on the economic cycle and the will of the employer. Employees were thankful to have a job, and employers often held all the cards. Economic stability and a strong pension were all businesses needed to get employees to show up and fulfill their life's journey of birth-school-work-death. Today, that's no longer all anyone's looking for.

In recent years, though, the power has shifted. Employer-based control of the equation has diminished, and loyalty has eroded as employees take personal responsibility to build a more secure future for themselves and their families. Employers who rely on certain talent groups, whether it's entry-level support roles or engineering and developer roles, report being "ghosted" by candidates who apply or interview but don't follow through on the hiring process—not showing up for interviews and sometimes not even calling back after they've received the message of a job offer. Similarly, newly hired employees sometimes drop out of the process without communication or decide to not show up on the first day of work. This behavior leaves the people who do the searching and hiring scratching their heads. It's easy to dismiss these behaviors as character flaws within those candidates. "Well,: employers might think," she must not have wanted the job so much after all, or he must be unreliable anyway," and maybe the employer dodged a bullet. But consider what else may be contributing. The fact is that as the employment market heats up and candidates have choices, they may be inclined to "live what they've learned" after years of bad behavior by employers during the recruiting process. While two wrongs don't make a right, the reality is that employees believe that the only obligation that they have is to pursue a path that meets their objective—which may be more than just earning a decent wage.

Just as consumers' attitudes have shifted, so have the attitudes of employees, which means that the employer brand has never been more important. The brand must have attributes, personality, and a certain texture that serves not only to attract the talent the company wants, but also stands as a promise that must be lived out every day. Companies must make good on these brands they're using to attract employees. In the best cases, every decision—from atmosphere and workspaces to engagement and social responsibility—will be part of this brand experience. The most successful companies have full buy-in, where each employee embraces why, how, and what the company stands for. As such, a clearly defined mission is a talent-attracting magnet that makes that company a destination for the like-minded.

Research continues to show that corporate America has an employee-engagement problem. A December 2017 Gallup poll estimates that more than 70 percent of all workers are disengaged.[3] Compare that number to data among those working for more mission-driven ventures such as nonprofits, where engagement levels skyrocket to 93 percent, according to a study published by Work for Good.[4] The data is clear: when organizations are anchored by purpose and mission, they become beacons for those who share their cultural values and productivity soars.

There are growing expectations that the patriarchal approach from employers of the past be replaced by a

---

3   *State of the American Workplace.* Gallup, Inc. December 2016. http://news.gallup.com/file/reports/199961/SOAW_Report_GEN_1216_WEB_FINAL_rj.pdf

4   "The Non-Profit Workforce Speaks," April 2018.

far more inclusive relationship—one where transparency and honesty are central and bringing value is nonnegotiable. For many employees, the job they inhabit today is merely a temporary vehicle providing utility based on what they value most at that moment. This has led to businesses categorizing millennials as fickle. We maintain that, rather than label or categorize a population negatively or get frustrated, it is imperative to make strategic adjustments to capitalize on the changing appetites. Though it's tempting to pass the blame on to millennials, they don't maintain an exclusive on this changing expectation of value. This attitude of looking at a career as a lattice instead of the age-old corporate ladder transcends generations as workers across the board now view their jobs more holistically. This more sophisticated approach to evaluating present and future roles says that employers are relevant only so long as they provide utility and/or personal growth as a stepping stone to whatever is next.

For many, the end goal is being in business for yourself—and the perceived freedom that comes with it. It is the reason that the gig economy in the United States has doubled every two years since 2014. Employers are no longer just competing for the loyalty of their own full-time employees but also against a burgeoning freelance economy. Businesses are being forced to ask themselves, "What will appeal to these new workers? A kick-ass and collaborative work space, lunch provided, college loan repayment, leadership development, or tools that help them build their own businesses?" The answer is yes—to all of these.

BOTTOM LINE

Modern workers view themselves as investible, and they prioritize organizations that will help them gain the necessary skills and experiences to propel them to the next level. For a growing number of people, the gig economy offers the best of both worlds—freedom and the flavor of entrepreneurism. Organizations that operate from a place of abundance instead of one of scarcity will embrace this reality by putting the right actions in place to meet the needs of employees and consumers alike.

REFLECT

1. How can you simulate certain entrepreneurial elements employees value within your business environment and turn those into a strategic advantage to your business? What may happen if you choose to stick with the status quo?
2. As an employee, how have your personal expectations for what you want out of our job—beyond simply a paycheck—changed?

CHAPTER 4

WHOLLY DIFFERENT

"Do you ever listen when I am talking to you?" The unmistakable South African voice on the other end of the line—which so happens to belong to my beautiful wife—irritatedly asks. "I told you three times we are going to the Breskals' house for dinner. You need to leave now because it's LA, and there WILL be traffic! Oh, and pick up a nice bottle of wine and some flowers?" Nonchalantly, I respond, "No problem, babe," knowing that anything else will serve to increase her ire, and because there is a Whole Foods around the corner where I can check all of the boxes and still reach my destination on time. In doing so, I elevate myself from a forgetful ass into a thoughtful dinner guest and an amazing husband. At least only my wife knows I almost forgot the dinner entirely, let alone that I wouldn't have shown up with flowers and wine unless she'd suggested it. Thank god for that Whole Foods.

THE EXPERIENTIAL GROCER

Whole Foods understands that this story plays out across its national footprint time and again. Their ability to capitalize on this shared experience is not only evident in their beautifully arranged flower displays and robust selection of both value-driven and high-end wines, but it also shows in the expertise of the specialists in each department. The knowledgeable wine specialists offer a recommendation based on your planned menu and provide you a story that you can retell as though you were reading through the expert pages of *Wine Spectator*. What could have been a stressful errand has turned into a delightful experience poised to become a potential topic of conversation at the dinner table. It not only ensures that the next time you're in a similar spot you'll definitely go back to Whole Foods, becoming more deeply rooted in their ecosystem, but also that you share your experience with their target demographic. Now, the next time your friends' spouses call them to remind them about a dinner party they'd forgotten, they're more likely to stop by Whole Foods, too.

The Whole Foods experience, and the consumer feelings that it evokes, is not all that different from the East-Coast-based chain Wegmans. Walking through their store is akin to undertaking a food odyssey, chock full of seemingly endless action stations to grab your attention and tantalize your taste buds. As soon as you enter your local Wegmans, you can't help but feel a blended sense of delight at all the choices and calm as the soft, yellow lighting soothes you. Now, your most challenging decision is which corner of this charming oasis you want to start in.

Walking past the immaculately displayed produce featuring plenty of organic options and fresh-cut medleys, you soon make your way to the crown jewel of the store. Here you meet an array of global cuisine options available to take, from sushi to Mexican food to hoagies and pizza. Got a hankering for something sweet? The open-air bakery provides all your favorites and then some—including their signature Ultimate Chocolate Cake and Ultimate Chocolate Chip Cookie. Everything they do is "Ultimate," not to be outdone. After making some selections, you stock up on a few essentials—all are Wegmans house brand, not because it is less expensive or you have coupons, but because you actually prefer the Wegmans house brand, which rarely has coupons. On your way out, you take stock of the plethora of inspirations and conveniences that will be waiting for another day—a bright and cheery catering office, a sophisticated wine shop with local selections, and delectable cheese displays featuring a menagerie of choices for every palate. Prominently situated in the store is a handsome, dark mahogany dining table decked out in seasonally appropriate décor, displayed in a manner that looks like it could have been ripped from the pages of *House Beautiful* magazine. Honorable mention also goes to the in-store floral studio, which offers sophisticated arrangements that would rival those in a five-star Manhattan hotel. Wegmans' mission is about "helping families live healthier, better lives through food," and everything they do from store aesthetics, to food selection, to conveniences is in service of that philosophy. When you walk through their doors, you feel it.

THE OTHER GUYS

You know what the opposite feels like too. We've all gone to that grocery store whose water-stained popcorn drop ceiling is interspersed with buzzing fluorescent lights that reflect a greenish hue off of the speckled linoleum floors. We struggle to push our wobbly-wheeled shopping carts through the maze of nonsensical aisles. Without the refrigerated units and partially stocked shelves, it would feel more like a hospital than a place to satiate the hunger pangs resulting from a night of fill-in-the-blank with your favorite brand of social pleasure. Overworked and under-inspired night shift employees appear one moment and seem to hide the next, almost like zombies of the apocalypse in their aimless roaming, inability to make eye contact, and incoherent grunts in response to even the most minor of customer inquiries. These stores survive only to serve those with no other choice—in a pinch for some milk and eggs or getting a jar of pickles and some ice cream in the middle of the night for their pregnant wife.

Consumers have many options even when it comes to ordinary grocery shopping. Whole Foods and Wegmans, in addition to niche markets such as Hispanic grocer Vallarta or Mituswa, which specializes in Asian products, understand that today's shoppers want authentic and experiential environments. It's no longer just about shopping lists and double coupons. The efficient Amazon Prime delivers commodities, sure, but Lighthouse retailers deliver experiences. They not only meet consumption needs but also inspire, educate, and delight...or give away free samples. This strategy has its upside. These retailers can charge a premium—which, if strong revenues are any indication, goes unnoticed by their consumers. After all, they have come to expect a reasonable mark-up as the price of admission.

LIGHTHOUSE DIFFERENTIATION

The contrasts between the metaphoric Lighthouse businesses and their Tugboat peers are fairly obvious across any number of industries we might consider here, but there are few that are as ubiquitous as the $5.35 trillion retail grocery business. In the United States in 2016, there were 38,441 retail supermarkets.[5] Undoubtedly, this is a crowded space. The most notable players are Kroger, who owns brands such as Ralphs, Fred Meyer, Food 4 Less, and Piggly Wiggly; Albertsons, whose purchase of Safeway now includes regional and national brands under the Randalls, Tom Thumb, Vons, Pavilions, ACME, and Jewel-Osco marquees; and Publix, who seems to dominate the Southeastern states. Yet mega companies like Walmart, disruptors like Amazon, niche players like Trader Joe's, and regional players like Wegmans continue to measurably change the game. They grab market share—forcing the old guard to consolidate for advantages-associated prices or reinvent themselves at great expense, usually with little measurable success. It would be unfair to cast aspersions on any of these prolific businesses, but all the same, we will attempt to point out what makes some prolific while it may be time for others to make a change before they end up in the retail grave-yard in which A&P, Eagle Food Centers, and Dominick's now reside.

The power in the compelling Whole Foods and Weg-

5   Thomas, Lauren. "With Whole Foods, Amazon Enters an Overcrowded Supermarket Space." CNBC. August 23, 2017. Accessed December 21, 2018. https://www.cnbc.com/2017/08/22/with-whole-foods-amazon-enters-an-overcrowded-supermarket-space.html.

mans examples is in their rightful place in the market as Lighthouse grocers. At their very core, Lighthouses have a defining mission and everything they do is about advancing that mission. Whole Foods and Wegmans live their missions. The consumers see that authenticity, and over time it's what makes them not casual shoppers but raving fans. If you ever meet someone from upstate New York, New Jersey, eastern Pennsylvania, or Maryland, they will eventually start talking about Wegmans.

Lighthouse businesses compel the people who experience what they have to offer to share it with others. It happens effortlessly. Just ask any Trader Joe's junkie what their favorite item is. You'll see their eyes light up as they recount the affordable wine selection, or the irresistible collection of frozen canapes, or their amazing selection of desserts. This enthusiasm extends beyond customers. Just as Starbucks made the barista "a thing," it's likely that you might sense some pride from a Trader Joe's team member. All of the brand elements working together creates something rather "hipster" around bagging groceries at Trader Joe's, more so than at your average supermarket. The mission creates attraction and staying power that draw in consumers and talent alike. When people interact with the organization that is genuine to its core, keeps its promises, and owns its mistakes, people appreciate that and reward it through their loyalty.

OPEN, GENUINE ENVIRONMENT

Working within a Lighthouse organization is special. As a key member of the team—which, notably, is a worthy designation ascribed to everyone—you have the freedom to be who you are and express your thoughts and ideas respectfully without fear of labeling or reprisal. The Lighthouse business affords this necessary luxury because it knows who it is as an organization and who it's not.

Unapologetic in its mission, Lighthouse leadership sources diverse talent with similar shared values. Therefore, any feedback, constructive criticism, or new idea is viewed through the lens of furthering the mission of the organization. There are other major benefits of this "all-in-it-together" mentality. This collective sense of ownership and collaboration often nips in the bud malignancies such as silos—individuals or teams working for their own ends, seeking credit rather than community or personal recognition rather a team win. Often, they prioritize their own areas of expertise or ability to make immediate impact, which leads to territorialism and a fear of sharing skills, projects, or priorities. The result is internal politics, inefficiency from a lack of communication, and an environment of fits and starts without any progress. Within Lighthouse organizations, a bevy of restrictive policies and rules or strict performance standards aren't as necessary, because people tend to police themselves and hold each other accountable. The fact is that you rarely need to hold people accountable to things they believe in.

EXPERIMENTATION AND INNOVATION

Successful Lighthouse businesses are far more insulated from environmental changes in the marketplace than their Tugboat counterparts. When the building plan for these structures is fortified by a solid foundation and quality material (both products and people), it operates from a highly sustainable place of strength, integrity, and credibility. The Lighthouse capacity for success is seemingly unlimited. They are beacons that emanate a very specific message to the marketplace. Clients and the best talent are attracted to the brightness of the mission. Lighthouse growth seems almost effortless, and these businesses tend to stand out on the shoreline above all others.

These well-constructed organizations stand tall amidst the sea of change because they are not reacting to that change; they are positioned for it and, in some cases, taking an active role in shaping it. Consider again the Whole Foods and Wegmans examples for a moment; as Lighthouse organizations, they surely noted the shifts in consumer attitudes when it came to health consciousness. What started as a gradual understanding of the modern food supply chain with its harmful pesticides, GMOs, and other undesirables grew into a return to locally sourced fruits and veggies from neighborhood farmer's markets and an interest in organic alternatives. Rather than digging their heels in the ground and offering more coupons, these stores and others like them jumped in early with experimentation to test consumer willingness to spend. They knew there was likely an interest in organic produce, but what about pasta sauce? Grass-fed beef? Cage-free chicken? Soon the idea of eating "whole foods" had become part of every health nut's vocabulary, and this strategic branding made the company synonymous with the product. Much like what Xerox did for copiers and Kleenex did for tissues, Whole Foods became a Lighthouse grocer for the ever-expanding market of those seeking to eat organic, local, and otherwise "whole" foods.

Lighthouses across industries are adopting this type of experimentation as part of their DNA. It isn't to say that they abandon what is working for some unproven "blue ocean" idea. Instead, Lighthouses recognize that every strategy, no matter how productive today, has a shelf life— or what we refer to as the **arc of effectiveness**.

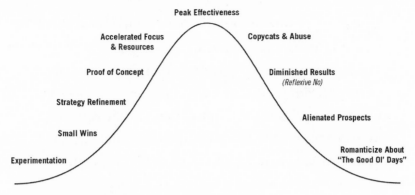

Peak Effectiveness

Accelerated Focus & Resources

Copycats & Abuse

Proof of Concept

Diminished Results
(Reflexive No)

Strategy Refinement

Alienated Prospects

Small Wins

Experimentation

Romanticize About "The Good Ol' Days"

* No actual scientific study was performed, and no animals were injured in the collection of this data.

Lighthouses aim to stay ahead of the arc, knowing that by the time the masses embrace a strategy or technique, the results are significantly diminished. Instead, these companies commit to embracing and shaping change that keeps them nimble and strong in the competitive environment.

360 DEGREE VALUE

Lighthouse organizations live and breathe their values. If they are focused on the experience and making consumer interaction enjoyable and pleasurable, then everything from the texture of the physical location or site, to the consistency and genuineness of the service, to the intuitiveness and personalization of your encounter looks effortless *because it is effortless*. These organizations aren't straining to be something that they aren't. Lighthouse organizations have taken an honest look at who they are. Instead of operating from the mentality of "What can we get away with?" they think about "What can we give away?" They are fiercely value-driven and realize that value is in the eye of the beholder—namely the consumer. So, they decide what their multi-prong value proposition looks like and then make use of that specific value-add, time and time again, in a way that is über-authentic and serves to delight prospective and existing consumers.

Our bold prediction: *only Lighthouse organizations will thrive in the modern marketplace.* The rest of the noise-makers are just treading water, like a rudderless tugboat adrift at sea, or worse, sinking to the bottom until they become irrelevant.

BOTTOM LINE

A monumental, irreversible shift has taken place in a market chock full of options that have measurably raised the expectations bar. As a metaphor for businesses who are reshaping the landscape, Lighthouses embrace exper-imentation and innovation while influencing consumer appetites. These risk-takers are in some cases redefining outdated industries and in other cases creating new ones. Ignoring the power of being at the tip of the spear will lead to certain failure and the demise of many businesses. But this reality brings with it a silver lining for those who figure it out.

REFLECT

1. How are Lighthouses positioned differently in your industry (or in general) than their Tugboat counterparts?
2. In addition to the grocery industry, what other examples can you identify where organizations are taking risks with innovation and experimentation?
3. Refer back to the Arc of Effectiveness diagram and consider where your business is in the cycle? Where can you initiate experimentation that could help you differentiate in the marketplace?

CHAPTER 5

SLUGGISH VESSEL

Consider the illustrative picture of a tugboat. While you might think back to the days when you read *Scuffy the Tugboat* as a kid and came to admire this fictional cartoon character's water adventures, no doubt you agree with the notion that the real-life vessels are far less charming. These transactional boats move slowly in and out of the harbor, compelled to deal with the crisis of the day.

The modern marketplace is littered with Tugboat-like organizations reacting to an array of crises and external competitive elements. In their attempts to navigate the fierce realities of sales, talent acquisition and retention, and innovation, Tugboats struggle with their limited capacity. They are unable to scale without debilitating organizational pain and huge expense (and more Tugboats). Client and talent acquisition are costly, time-consuming, and extremely difficult. So, they predictably conduct business by moving one ship (prospect, account, recruit) at a time, often against great headwind. These are the businesses who respond to consumers' Reflexive Nos with more and more noise.

Tugboats are exposed to both mechanical and human failure. Many become so reliant on the expertise and execution of their captains (leaders) that Tugboats try hard to retain these people, often by creating a comfortable place for them to stay. While retention efforts are practical, when too much emphasis is placed on a small contingent at the top, these leaders can easily become unchecked in their ineffectiveness or apathy, which compounds the sluggish, transactional nature of the business. What's worse is when the continued presence of these leaders at the helm creates a false sense of comfort. This set-it-and-forget-it mindset can manifest itself through complacency around succession planning to ensure that the company is cultivating its next generation of leaders who will bring fresh energy and ideas.

Working for a hapless Tugboat business is a grind. There's a major disconnect between the image that the company projects externally when compared to what it's actually like on the inside. The "inside" is all too commonly a dizzying array of confusion due to a lack of clear vision, personal agendas, red tape, propped-up mediocre performers, codes of silence, sacred cows, and other BS minutia that encompasses "the way things are done around here." If you are currently stuck in a Tugboat environment, these attributes are all too familiar, and it is downright exhausting.

LIP SERVICE

Tugboat businesses are major proponents of lip service. Leaders within these firms will say things like, "top-tier talent is essential to our growth" and that they "value diverse perspectives," and yet they make a thousand decisions every day that sit in stark contrast to these statements. The disconnect lies in the fact that the way Tugboat businesses approach talent is inefficient and time-consuming.

When these organizations need talent, they fire up the recruiting engines, make their way out of their harbors (Indeed, Career Builder, The Ladders, Zip Recruiter, or Craigslist), identify candidates, and pull them in. As if this kind of churn wasn't strenuous enough, when you add a bad recruiter or a process breakdown or technology failure to the mix, it only compounds the problem. A potential job applicant is lucky if they are actually able to advance through that murky process, which really isn't a process so much as it is a charade that leaves people feeling disenchanted and treated like cattle. This "process" may include being filtered by an impersonal applicant-tracking system encounter, a "phone screen" interview with someone who knows nothing about the job itself, a series of personality tests, IQ tests, background checks, reference checks, hiring manager interviews, team member interviews, conversations with Cathy down the hall (not sure what she even does), HR conversations, and the Big Boss who has carved out five minutes for the ceremonial handshake and idle chatter about "how important this position is to the organization" (without much more detail than that). By the time you reach the finish line, you're seriously considering if you want to work alongside these unspectacular people anyway.

By contrast, Lighthouse organizations believe that strong talent is critical to their organization, and so they never stop identifying talent—even when no position is currently open. The consensus belief system throughout the organization is that the company with the best talent wins—and so everyone is always on the lookout. The janitor is just as likely to extend the hand of opportunity to someone they come into contact with as the HR person or the CEO. Everyone shares a relentless pursuit of upgrading talent, and there is a set of actions that align with this way of thinking across the entire recruiting and talent-development life cycle. The clarity of a Lighthouse business's understanding of its mission serves as a talent magnet. People are drawn to the organization not because of the business they are in, but because the organization knows why it exists and why people sincerely matter to the equation. Prospective talent feels this throughout the full duration of the recruiting experience, and even if they don't end up being offered a job, they leave with a great fondness for the organization because they were treated with respect throughout each interaction.

Beyond recruiting and hiring, many Tugboats have an archaic approach toward "talent management." Arbitrary metrics loaded into a crappy, ill-designed talent management portal collect and score irrelevant attributes to provide a feedback loop and ranking that is often directly correlated to compensation. Instead of lending truthful feedback, these systems are manipulated to perpetuate cronyism or silence the squeaky wheel. Equally alarming is that top-down pressure requiring these procedures be executed leaves thoughtful leaders hamstrung—forced to assign numbers they don't believe are fair to people on their team. Worst of all, these managers have to endure the further indignity of trying to explain the unexplainable to their team members.

Similarly, some Tugboats establish performance goals that no employee, no matter how talented, could possibly achieve because of internal personnel and resource obstacles that make rolling a boulder up a mountain seem a far more worthwhile pursuit. For example, let's say you have an employee who is in a Manager of Client Support role and is very good at process. One of the performance goals for the year might be to design and then lead the execution of a sales-through-service process that will accelerate certain key activities like product demos, proposals, legal sign-off, and implementation kick-off. Even if the process is perfectly designed, there are factors outside of their control when it comes to adoption. Even if the service side gets fully on board, what if the sales team or the sales leader refuses to adhere to the process? When leadership up the food chain is solicited for support, that request is met with the standard response: "don't make too many waves, because the salespeople have to focus on making their quotas."

The challenges arise at performance reviews time. What kind of feedback and ratings do you think this employee will need to grin and bear? (Hint: It won't be good. He didn't meet his goal!) Of course, this is one out of an infinite number of other ridiculous examples, so why stick with these outdated performance reviews? The answers: "They've always existed before to create expectations and accountability," or "We've invested a great deal of money," or "How else can we quantify performance within a standardized non-discriminatory way?" Or so the story goes. The irony is that these processes are demotivating, costly, and anything but standardized or non-discriminatory.

Tugboat organizations are also addicted to a faulty feedback loop that placates their ego and allows them to publicly brag about being one of the "Best Places to Work" while perpetuating the status quo. Often, they have entire departments dedicated to this work. They spend their days designing and interpreting employee engagement surveys that deliver the answers that they want from the outset. When the information is not aligned, it gets ignored, buried, or dismissed as the byproduct of a bad sample. This is just the right amount of faulty evidence to perpetuate the delusion within the C-Suite. Meanwhile, decisions are made that further erode the culture and morale of the organization. Tugboat companies will perpetuate a story about never having layoffs, yet they regularly recategorize a population or eliminate a role without any reasonable explanation. The result is everyone is concerned that they may be next. The same Tugboat companies that pat themselves on the back for delivering record profits to shareholders simultaneously pontificate about needing to cut expenses—budgets are restrained and compensation and bonus plans are altered. They eliminate many of the perks or events that once were the core of their culture and turn others into solemn versions of what once was. They increase auditing and reject what used to be standard expenses under the banner of diligence. This austerity erodes the culture.

Conversely, Lighthouse organizations don't get caught

up in the stifling nature of performance reviews, or wait for employee engagement surveys to deliver their unsurprising verdicts, or waste energy or money perpetuating a false narrative of the reality. Instead these organizations focus on fashioning an environment built on trust and a common goal. They tackle challenges together and are committed to one another. Leadership understands that when the people do well, the company does well. This creates pride in the outfit and an openness to both delivering and receiving feedback.

Again, much is made about feedback, but let's not kid ourselves. If feedback isn't cloaked in trust, it feels like an iron fist with a ribbon around it: it might have the appearance of a gift, but it hurts like hell. Lighthouse businesses use continuous top-down, bottom-up, and peer-to-peer feedback as a means of bringing out the best in each other. They understand that on some level, you don't need to hold people accountable to things they believe in and nurturing an environment that perpetuates this is paramount. This mentality leads to a feeling that everyone is being treated as an adult. Does this work for everyone? No. But it works for Lighthouse businesses and for those who were meant to lead them and support them as members of their teams.

CANDOR NON-GRATA

Specific to the topic of feedback, another pervasive issue of Tugboat business is their low—or, in many cases, lack of—tolerance for candor. What these leaders fail to realize is that candor is the glue that holds high-functioning organizations together. Instead, Tugboats are repelled by it.

This aversion to candor plays out in a few ways. One of the most cancerous is through retaliation. Most organizations have their share of wise heretics. These are people who have either been inside long enough to see history perpetually repeat itself or they bring a fresh perspective either through being an outsider or because of their youth. Often, these sages will voice their observations and concerns as thoughtful disagreement. After getting the token nod or empty thanks while nothing changes, many of them will simply start to accept that "this is the way it is here." However, there's always that especially bold remnant who will keep the commentary (and criticism) going. These are the game-changers, the ones who can move the Tugboat organization to rethink and reimagine themselves as a Lighthouse. They are also the ones at the greatest risk of getting targets placed on their backs by those who feel threatened by their perspectives and growing influence.

In an effort to silence the dissension, Tugboat leaders will dispatch tools for dealing with these "rogue troublemakers." When possible, they will attempt to diminish these people's influence through public character assassination, passive-aggressive posturing, or outright blacklisting. In their final stand, they will make it clear to all that they are drawing a line in the sand to find out whose side people are on, using positional authority and fear to stave off the wave of opposition. They will use the old trusty performance review, where words like "difficult," "doesn't get along with others," or any other thinly veiled, subjective critiques sneak their way into this supposedly objective tool. Candor requires organizations to set aside the carnival mirrors to look at what is really playing out each and every day. In a sea clouded with personal agendas and hampered by rigid spans of control, candor threatens the status quo, and it must be suppressed.

The allergic response to candor also plays out through the worship of sacred cows—ideas that are so ingrained in the culture that to question them seems like heresy. Like personal agendas, sacred cows are a major issue for Tugboat organizations. When allowed to roam unquestioned, a sacred cow can range from being a disconnection to a distraction to an actual destabilizer. They can manifest themselves in the form of an individual or team within the company that is "off-limits" for scrutiny to a project or favorite idea. Everyone knows what a sacred cow looks like. It requires constant praise and adoration and never any criticism or questioning of its relevance or importance. In fact, if you must speak up with anything resembling contrariness to the status quo, you better walk on eggshells and choose your words and tones carefully, being as tactful as possible.

There are countless examples of these sacred cows—from spending exorbitant amounts of budget dollars on pet projects that create no differentiation, to fruitless advertising campaigns driving metrics that have little to no measurable ROI, to people inhabiting unjustifiable legacy positions or who are allowed to sunset their careers as "consultants" doing little more than collecting their paychecks.

NOTHING TO SEE HERE

When the leaders of Tugboat organizations exhibit a "do as I say, not as I do" management style, it's nothing but empty calories and does not feed employee engagement. This includes spouting popular buzzwords like "accountability" and "ownership" of areas of responsibility. People often feel a visceral negative response to this empty talk, because rather than create a culture of consistency where the leader also holds himself or herself to the same standards, they instead use words as tools of control. Imagine a Tugboat leader who loves to talk about excellence and how he wants it to play out in every facet of the organization's life. Meanwhile, this same guy regularly shows up for internal meetings unprepared and frazzled yet ready to hijack the agenda to redirect the session toward wherever his head is at the moment. The team is continually left in a perpetual state of paralysis and confusion about how best to proceed. Any real candor about this problem would be about as welcome as a jackhammer outside the window at 3:00 a.m.

Lighthouse organizations take the business of hiring and promoting people into leadership roles as a very serious matter. They are careful in their pursuits, because they realize that these leaders need to be as authentic as the mission itself. There's no room for double-standards or hypocrisy. People can smell that stench a mile away. Instead, Lighthouse leaders are among the most other-centered within the whole enterprise. They model the behaviors they want to see in others first, and when they mess up, they own it. That level of transparency and genuineness may not win any perfectionism awards or create any good old-fashioned ego boosts, but it does create waves including waves of respect from those bearing witness to this style of leadership.

STALE ROMANCE

Another signature characteristic of the Tugboat business is their love affair with the past. In a marketplace where everything has changed, these stubborn organizations want to bemoan the glory days and stick with what they have always been doing. If they do make a change, it's minimal and way too slow to matter.

Look no further than the rash of retail closures in recent years. These were once the titans of industry, but now their hollow shops sit as vacant reminders of what happens when businesses fail to adapt. It's too easy an answer to say that consumer behavior was the sole reason for the demise of these retail chains. While that is one factor, the far bigger issue was these stores' inability to engage them in a meaningful way and present options and opportunities to capture their attention and their wallets.

Think about a services-based organization in a crowded market that has always competed primarily on efficiency and price. While this may be a winning mix to a point, this company is out there fighting for share on price and a promise of speed, but their people are simply a cog in the system and will eventually move on to an organization where they have the chance to be connected to the mission and an integral part of that business's purpose. Now this services business is stuck in Tugboat mode because— beholden to a low-price provider model—they're chasing consumers and pining after talent. It's exhausting, time-consuming, and, as history tells us, unsustainable. Like the many retailers before them, this services business is on a dangerous collision course.

Lighthouse organizations recognize that experimentation is the antidote to extinction. Though they're mission-driven, they are agile and realize that delivering value is king. However, just as consumer attitudes are continuously changing, so is how consumers perceive value. So, Lighthouse businesses stay close to the consumer, building connections with them, learning from them, and adapting to them. It's not a "consumer habits" research and insights study they undertake every five years but an ongoing business strategy. It's one that pays off, because a Lighthouse organization is a relentless listening organization.

BOTTOM LINE

LIGHTHOUSE BUSINESSES

Monitor what has worked and watch for declining ROI

Experiment constantly (advertising, marketing, distribution) and are fearless pioneers

Not only encourage creativity and candor at every level, but expect it

Refuse to make excuses

Remain steadfastly committed to ensuring that their brand is synonymous with value, innovation, and integrity

Strive to make loyalists of all employees, even those who choose to leave

LIGHTHOUSE TEAM MEMBERS ARE:

Invested in the overall success of the organization; when the company wins, they win

Given the opportunity for meaningful contributions

Encouraged to pursue their passions, even if they are outside of the company—the organizational/ team member relationship is viewed as more important that holding them hostage

TUGBOAT BUSINESSES

Stick with what worked before (advertising, marketing, distribution)

Fearful of experimentation

Discourage creativity

Remain romantic about the past

Punish heresy or worse, ignore it

IN A TUGBOAT ENVIRONMENT, EMPLOYEES ARE:

Paid for a specific task, not the value they bring

Developed largely through programs for mass consumption

Viewed as replaceable while being saddled with things like non-compete agreements

REFLECT

1. Which Tugboat beliefs or behaviors do you recognize within your organization?
2. How do these beliefs or behaviors weaken the organization within the competitive landscape?
3. Does your organization's talent practices reflect those associated with Tugboats or Lighthouses?

PART 2

MISSION CONTROL

CHAPTER 6

THE ANATOMY OF AUTHENTICITY

In early 2009, I moved to Southern California from Chicago in pursuit of a new opportunity. Many lifestyle adjustments lay in store, and numerous tasks needed to be completed before my wife could join me with our two-year-old daughter and our soon-to-be-born son. I needed to find a place for us to live, sign a lease on a new office space, and donate all of my winter clothes to the Salvation Army. In Chicago, my wife and I shared a BMW X5 that was both practical for the weather and for getting groceries in style. But as the song goes, "Nobody walks in LA," and not being able to share a car opened a window of opportunity to buy the car I'd been dreaming of since the 2006 Chicago Auto Show—the Maserati Gran Sport.

Luckily, a friend who worked at Ferrari of Newport Beach—and my wife not being present to encourage practicality—set the stage for me to buy this beautiful, handmade Italian stunner. And I did so without even the token test drive. In fact, I arrived by airplane and headed straight to the dealership to sign some papers and pick up the keys. From the minute I drove off the lot, I knew I had made the right decision. Anyone who has driven a Maserati (and not the mass-produced Ghibli, which drives more like a Chrysler than a Ferrari) will describe the way it makes them feel. They will exalt the architects who successfully combine flawless, appointed leather stylings that scream superb Italian craftsmanship with the guttural roar of its unmistakable engine just begging you to push this machine to its limits. Car enthusiasts will most certainly tell you that they fell in love with the aggressive lines that make the car appear as though it were traveling at 200 mph when standing still.

But not everything about Maserati is brag-worthy. I came to realize this about two weeks into owning my new car when an intermittent squealing led me right back to the dealer. As Murphy's Law would have it, anything that could go wrong did. The technician could not get the car to make the noise I'd heard, so he sent me on my way and told me to come back if it happened again. No more than two miles from the service center, the sound reappeared. I whipped the car around and headed right back to the dealer. This time, though, I stayed in the car with him.

As we pulled out of the lot, there it was: *eerreeeeeshhhhh-hprrrrrrreeeek.* Proof that I was not crazy.

Like a prideful toddler, I exclaimed, "You hear it?" He quickly jerked the steering wheel all the way to the left and punched the gas. The sound disappeared, and the technician said, "It was likely just a loose bearing. Problem solved." I looked at him, somewhat perplexed, and asked, "Is this a common issue?" To which he replied "Sir, there are fewer than 2,500 of these cars in the whole world. Each of them was made by hand, and because of that, they make noises. It is all part of the charm of owning a Maserati. If you want something that doesn't make noise, you can buy a Mercedes or a Porsche, but it won't be nearly as much fun!"

You see, Maserati is unapologetically self-aware of who they are and what they believe. They seem to have ignored the actions of other luxury brands who have focused on smart technology, fuel efficiency, and other trends. Instead they, by their own decree, seek to "build ultra-luxury performance automobiles with timeless Italian style, accommodating bespoke interiors, and effortless, signature sounding power."

Loyalists like me vigorously defend against this philosophy to those who besmirch the brand for its shoddy "infotainment" system, which is five years behind the times. I just smile and tell them all, "It's a sacrifice I am willing to make. Besides, if the sound system was better, I couldn't hear the engine."

Maserati seems to suggest that if you want an engine that roars and a handsome, custom leather-appointed interior, "We are the obvious choice," and if you want technology, well, buy a Tesla! In the end, Maserati understands that staying true to its identity in an authentic way speaks directly to its target audience, who is searching for exactly what they deliver. As a result, Maserati owners proudly join clubs, buy merchandise, and proselytize in a manner that encourages like-minded souls to join the tribe of those unified under the distinctive trident emblem.

THE IMPORTANCE OF AUTHENTICITY

A lot of people struggle with the concept of authenticity. Some define it as being unapologetic about the way you speak or behave. Others fixate on origins, pontificating about the past and how their experience is foundational to their true self. More than likely, the first version of authenticity is just an excuse to be a narcissistic asshole, while the second leaves no path to clarity for those seeking to manifest it strategically within their businesses.

What is certain is that we all know what *inauthenticity* looks and sounds like. It's when you're sitting across from someone who is so full of bullshit that all you can hear is the sound of Charlie Brown's teacher's voice. It's also that gut feeling you have the moment you perceive that an influencer's endorsement is solely predicated on a monetary payment. Or, when we find out that the holier-than-thou preacher who relentlessly spoke about the sin of others makes the front-page news for adultery, or worse, his collection of kiddie-porn.

Within the context of the Lighthouse philosophy, authenticity is about alignment of mission with actions. It means leaders and businesses staying true to their ideals and remembering who they serve. It's about both having the integrity to always strive to do what you say you are going to and owning it when you fall short. In our modern day of discerning customers and perceptive employees, businesses and the leaders within them no longer have the option to represent themselves in anything other than an honest, transparent, and authentic way. Ironically enough, if they're not being transparent, people will see right through them.

Increasingly, we've collectively come to expect businesses to behave more like people. We expect those with whom we have relationships to have certain qualities and characteristics. In fact, a 2017 survey conducted by Stackla found that nearly 90 percent of millennials, 85 percent of Gen Xers, and 80 percent of Boomers claimed that "authenticity is important to them when deciding which brands to support."[6] The survey further noted that 57 percent of those surveyed felt that less than half of all brands represented themselves authentically, which as many as 30 percent reported as a leading factor in their decisions to abandon brands they'd once supported. Authenticity is crucial to continued loyalty from fickle audiences.

When effectively deployed and maintained, authenticity is the DNA for your enterprise's identity. It gives you substance beyond the transaction itself—the buying and selling—and that sense of realness and purpose besides just making the sale leads to consumer relatability, trust, and loyalty. It encourages engagement, increases your influence, and can turn your audience into advocates who help perpetuate the brightness of your mission.

A SIMPLE RECIPE

If you want to rise above the competition to become a Lighthouse—whether you're starting from scratch or reimagining your business in a new light—there are some fundamental qualities to consider. You can't create a culture of authenticity overnight, but if you do put in the work, it will pay huge dividends in the long run.

---

6 "Why UGC Is The Key To Authenticity & Consumer Influence." Stackla. May 18, 2018. Accessed December 21, 2018. https://stackla.com/resources/blog/why-ugc-is-key-to-authenticity-consumer-influence/.

We suggest the following: **Be Real.** It's amazing how many businesses and their leaders get this wrong. To be great in the marketplace, it isn't enough to claim to be something—you have to actually be it. Being real starts from a place of deep passion that results in a definable set of goals and a clearly stated mission (we'll get to that in the next chapter). This should stay front-of-mind and central to your strategy at all times. To ensure realness, ask yourself:

- Who do you aspire to be as a business?
- Who do you aspire to be as an employer, leader, or employee?
- Are your actions and the stakeholder experiences aligned with these ideals?

Being willing to undertake this type of reflection is the first step on the path to separating yourself from the abundance of fakers standing in front of Lamborghinis they don't own, purporting to have the secret to manufacturing success in just two hours a day.

Be Consistent. Inconsistency is the fastest way to annihilate perceptions of authenticity. It smacks of contradiction, like a liar who can't keep his story straight. Inconsistency leads to suspicion and mistrust with both internal and external stakeholders. This is particularly important when we are talking about accessibility, alignment with brand expectation, creative content, and communication. There must be consistency in terms of quality and frequency. This is not to suggest that you need to treat everyone inside your organization or all clients the same. In fact, I have long maintained that I try to be as fair as possible by treating everyone differently. I am public and transparent about this people policy—I invest disproportionately where it is the obvious choice. Anyone can become the obvious choice at any time. *That* is my consistency. Figure out yours, and do not waiver.

Be Accessible. Most company founders and CEOs start off with open door policies that evaporate when profitability and success skyrocket. But in becoming less available, these leaders lose their connectedness to what's really going on in their businesses while simultaneously eroding public opinion to the point where others see them as self-important inauthentic douchebags. So, don't let your head get too big!

Remain accessible and nurture relationships with your stakeholders so they stay enthusiastic and engaged. This will prove extremely valuable in building authentic and lasting connections. When possible, actively engage with customers and employees in one-on-one settings. When this isn't possible, host meet-and-greets, where you set a time to bring small groups in and get to know them. Ask probing questions and listen to the answers. You'll gain valuable intel to solve problems before they escalate, and you'll keep your finger on the pulse of perspectives that shape employee attitudes toward you and the company.

Augment actual accessibility with virtual accessibility by giving customers and employees behind-the-scenes access through media. Produce videos, live streams, blogs, and whatever else you can think of to offer your team access to insights that they wouldn't otherwise get to share. Give them the benefit of your expertise and experience—for free. Include occasional glimpses into your personal life without divulging every detail (and seriously, stay away from political rants!). This combination of sharing your knowledge and sharing your personality will allow you to tactfully position yourself as a trustworthy authority in your industry, which both increases your credibility and allows your authenticity to shine through.

Be Generous. As it pertains to the aforementioned accessibility, we are talking about generosity with your time. However, there also increasing expectations that businesses do more than just count their profits. Organizations that dedicate themselves to a specific philanthropic cause in earnest win over time. This is more than writing a check or sponsoring a puppy adoption. It is about becoming a champion with a goal of real impact. When these endeavors are consistently undertaken and promoted, they help build *esprit de corps* among employees while winning over consumers who attribute altruistic qualities to you and your brand. This makes you more likable and relatable, and it ensures that you meet the expectations of both consumers and employees who believe businesses should espouse the same kinds of qualities we look for in the people with whom we build and maintain friendships or partnerships.

There is an added bonus to all this too, which hardly anyone thinks about. With true authenticity comes a sense of liberation and freedom. Being true to yourself and your business and being honest with the marketplace—including your prospective customers and employees—relieves the anxiety associated with faking it. It frees up the energy you'd be wasting on maintaining a facade. That energy boost, stress relief, and overall liberation can have a huge impact on a business as a whole, turning it into a real, genuine power to be reckoned with.

BOTTOM LINE

Some will, some won't—so what? The tough truth about authenticity is that it is unlikely you'll be everyone's cup of tea. People worry, "What if the market doesn't respond well to this real, true me?" But the upshot is that this is an incredibly liberating place from which to operate. The Lighthouse philosophy mandates that you stand tall upon an immovable foundation of authentic identity, which ensures that you are recognizable among all who are searching for you and others who happen upon you by mistake. Appreciate the full value of knowing who you are, and don't sweat the rest.

REFLECT

1. What are the trademarks of brands you perceive as authentic?
2. What do you want people to believe about you or your business?
3. If you were to ask someone who knows you and isn't your greatest fan, what would they say?
4. What is the disconnect between who you are, what you believe, and how you do business?

CHAPTER 7

THE PLUS-PLUS EQUATION

In West Los Angeles, there is a bake shop called Cookie Good. While on its face, Cookie Good may look like simply a gourmet bakery, they are really in the business of time travel. Cookie Good is about transporting you back to your childhood, back when you didn't have a worry in the world. A time when your greatest anxiety and stress was predicated on if Wile E. Coyote would get flattened by a falling anvil or take a tumble off a cliff before landing in a cloud of dust. A time when you based your decision about what to eat for breakfast not on nutritional value but on the quality of the sugar-milk that would remain in the bowl after the cereal was gone. Cinnamon Toast Crunch was my go-to favorite.

According to their website, Cookie Good's goal "was to create a space that was fun and familiar, yet clean and new; where the smiles of the people working behind the counter were as warm and inviting as the incredible smell of cookies baking inside; where kids and curious grown-ups could walk up to a glass wall and peer into the 40-quart mixer churning out batch after batch of dough." Within that space, they set out to "make cookies that not only taste amazing but also feed your soul; that make you remember something wonderful." They achieve this through a simple storefront that juxtaposes a showcase array of cookies and brownie bars against a white backdrop. Daily specials include flavors like Fruity Pebbles, Pancakes & Bacon, S'mores, Cheetos, and more. If they stopped here, they likely would be tasty, yes, but mostly unremarkable; it is their commitment to nostalgia that makes them a Lighthouse. In what we will refer to as their plus-plus, behind the Cookie Good sales counter sits a drink bubbler containing a full selection of after-milk (you remember, the milk left in the bowl after you got done eating the cereal). That's right, Cocoa Krispies, Crunch Berries, Cinnamon Toast Crunch, and Golden Grahams milk can be had by the glass or as a sample offered up in a plastic shot glass. It is unlikely that it is a money-maker, because anyone who drank more than an ounce would probably end up sick or with the worst sugar hangover of their life. However, this fancy milk is definitely part of the mystique and experience, and they generously give out shots to anyone interested in being transported back to their own ages of innocence.

MISSION CRITICAL

It seems almost too obvious to emphasize the significance of a clear vision and mission for an organization, but when we say "mission," we mean much more than just some inspirational guiding principles readymade for inscription upon a plaque to adorn your lobby wall.

A Lighthouse mission isn't just a simple ideal worth pursuing. It's predicated instead on a deep-rooted authentic identity. It requires a specific objective that concentrates energy around the value that you bring to the marketplace and serves as a litmus test separating what is important from what is not. It binds all stakeholders together around a common, well-defined goal. This mission is the light that emanates into the darkness attracting consumers and talent alike.

The best Lighthouse missions are rooted in solving simple problems or ideas and pay special attention to customer and employee experience. These missions are always articulated in a crisp and clean format designed to resonate with clients and talent. The hallmarks of a Lighthouse-worthy mission answer these questions:

- Why does the business exist?
- What value do you bring?
- What makes the business special?
- What value do you add (to consumers and employees)?

Each of these questions is important. And in case you are wondering, no, the answer to the first question is not "to make money." That is an outcome, but not a reason. A business's reason for existing should center around the consumer need or a problem that it solves.

That first question, why exist, is an essential starting point, but the rubber really meets the road in your answers to the next two questions.

To consider what makes you special is really to consider what makes you stand out. What is your secret sauce? If someone were to line you up next to five of your competitors, what would make you memorable?

The answer to this question should not be simply that you offer the lowest price. Using price as your only means of competitive differentiation is a dangerous game. You could be a dollar store, but what happens when along comes the 99 cents store? An identity that rests on lowest price is a Tugboat business fiercely fighting for share all while precariously traversing shallow waters where they will likely run aground.

The last question builds upon your differentiation to isolate, harness, and exploit the value that your business brings. What's your above-and-beyond? It's how you combine these things—parlaying your organization's reason for existence, *plus* your unique differentiation, *plus* how you go above and beyond—and weave them together to form an authentic tapestry of a mission that will attract consumers and talent to your organization. We call this **nailing your plus-plus**, as the Cookie Good example demonstrates so flawlessly. Their plus-plus is not that they are an amazing bake shop or even that they serve after-milk; it's that they trade in an experience that returns you to a happy place, a time when your biggest worry was what cartoon you'd watch after *Tom and Jerry*. Regardless of what industry you are in, this is your first task in transforming into a Lighthouse.

Tugboat businesses often mount a convincing effort to be missional in their behavior and actions but, in practice, they often confuse their idealistic vision for their operational reality. They get stuck in a myopic transaction mode focused on bottom-line profit over everything else and never deliver their plus-plus. This likely served them well in the past, delivering economic viability and perhaps industry prominence. In good times, these businesses may even have gotten close to fulfilling their promises to every set of their stakeholders, from their consumers to their employees to their shareholders. But as the winds change and the stormy seas of the brave new world have taken hold, the Tugboat captains revert to what is comfortable. Stricken with fear, they drop anything that resembles being additive—suggesting theses ideals are a luxury of economics instead of a necessity for survival. They batten down the hatches and focus on the other Tugboats in the harbor—competitors—and imitate their actions instead of setting their own course. The captains of these Tugboats suggest strategies under the banner of "going back to the basics." They talk about "blocking and tackling," abandoning experimentation in pursuit of "what has always worked." They fail to realize that reverting back to the same ol' thing will not necessarily get you the same results that you once got. When they combine this with tightening the purse strings and focusing purely on bottom-line profit, they alienate the very people who were drawn to what is now revealed to be a half-hearted mission.

BOTTOM LINE

In order to become a Lighthouse business, your mission must be more than a declarative statement of idealism; instead, it must serve as the foundation of the organization and the central reason for its existence. Not all missions need to be aspirational or inspirational, but they do need to authentically communicate what makes the organization special and clearly articulate the value it delivers both externally and internally. The plus-plus is often what differentiates one competitor from the other. It is what speaks to the marketplace and makes the Lighthouse easily distinguishable in the fog of the competition. To the Tugboat businesses lost at sea, there is a warning: evolve or suffer the consequences.

REFLECT QUESTIONS

1. As you evaluate your mission, can you answer these three questions:
    A. Why does the business exist?
    B. What makes the business special? (Your first plus in the plus-plus equation.)
    C. What value do you add to both consumers and employees? (Your second plus.)
2. Can you consolidate your plus-plus (your answers to the last two questions) into a mission statement?

CHAPTER 8

MISSION AS TRUE NORTH

As a child, I recall searching the horizon at dusk for a pillar that shot from the sand toward the darkening sky. With a boat full of the day's bounty from an off-shore fishing excursion, my job was to locate the beam of light to which we would aim our boat for safe passage. The Barnegat Lighthouse on the north end of Long Beach Island, New Jersey was easily distinguishable. As a rather utilitarian structure, the tower had a white base that changed to red brick halfway to the top before transitioning back to white up near the lens room. Though this lighthouse lacked some of the black-and-white majesty displayed up and down the barber shop pole structure that I had seen in Cape Hatteras, North Carolina, I could always count on its role in guiding me to safety. Another favorite for me was the must-see lighthouse on Fire Island. Its sand-dune aesthetic and red-roofed keeper's quarters-turned-museum delights tourists and residents alike. Juxtaposed against its own unique geographical back-drops, each of the lighthouses were strikingly different in appearance yet fundamentally and functionally the same. As physically imposing structures, their purpose was to safely guide all the mariners who were searching for them to the harbors and shorelines upon which they stood.

Just like the magnificent towers they are metaphorically compared to, Lighthouse businesses may look and feel different, but what they share in common is a defined mission and purpose. Lighthouses are all-in businesses. The value-driven mission that guides them is not only the force behind a Lighthouse's message to the market and for underwriting the value proposition to its talent, but that mission is central to the way the business operates.

Real lighthouses are designed with a main tower that con-nects the foundation to the light at the top. The strength of the foundation and main tower are critical to the structural integrity of the lighthouse. Both components mutually rely upon the other to ensure that the lighthouse is able to accomplish its purpose. Inside a Lighthouse business, the mission is the rock-solid foundation. That mission is *also* hardwired into the operating system of the business, its main tower. As the business functions each day, every action must advance the mission. That mission is so vital to the health and well-being of the business that it becomes the great filter for all decision-making. When weighing a potential option, the organization leads with the question, "If we say yes/no to this, will it power or diminish our Lighthouse?" They prioritize their structural integrity—emphasis on *integrity*.

Too many businesses operate superficially, making decisions without considering the possible ramifications of a change and what it might ultimately do to their organization. These Tugboats play the imitation game by projecting a veneer of who they want to be or who they think the market wants them to be. Most often, it's because they want to attract clients. In doing so, the Tugboat organization will bring their A-team to a sales pitch, armed with slick PowerPoint decks and glossy one-sheets. They turn up the charm and promise the moon, all in an effort to portray themselves as the perfect choice for the prospective client. All too often, these impressive bigshots who just won the big gig are off to their next sales conquest, handing off the client they just won over to the B, C, and yes, D team on their way out the door.

WHY DOES THIS HAPPEN?

The disconnect between the shiny face an organization puts on during the sales process and the everyday reality of what the client actually gets can be massive. Meanwhile, as the original A-team cashes their commission checks, dissatisfaction blooms within the clients they just won, and suddenly the client's business is on the verge of being lost just as quickly as it was won. This impending reality sounds the alarm, and now it's an all-hands-on-deck exercise to fix the problems. They deploy a menagerie of "retention strategies," which are really just Band-Aids. By the time they get it fixed, profit margins are shrinking, the client's initial confidence in the company has eroded, and competitors have an open door to exploit. Worst of all, this failed interaction negates any opportunity for the business to magnify its mission through the client extolling its virtues and overall experience—the ultimate goal of every interaction. It's hard to emphasize a fulfillment of a promise when you're in damage-control mode. When this cycle continues repeating itself, it becomes very destabilizing. If Tugboat operators find themselves always patching holes and flushing water off the deck, they simply cannot focus on the brightness of the mission.

PERCEIVED AND ACHIEVED CREDIBILITY

In today's environment, consumers have access to so much information that they've already formed a perception of your business by the time they walk through the doors. We call this reality-based consumerism. The fact is that if you have made it in front of a prospective client, you can rest assured that they have relentlessly researched your business and you. If they didn't like what they found, you probably wouldn't have gotten the meeting in the first place. So, there is no need to overdo it. Making fictitious assertions or embellishing during your initial interaction will destroy your perceived credibility, which will be disastrous for your achieved credibility.

For the purposes of deepening our conversation, let's define *credibility* as the quality of being trustworthy, reliable, and competent to such a degree that one's efforts are not met with skepticism and disregard. Credibility is a large and loaded concept, and it's important to dissect it further into two types:

- *Perceived credibility* is the credibility you have already gained or lost before you even open your mouth. This is based on what people believe to be true about you and the company you represent due to your reputation and relationships. It is also based on their experiences, observations, assumptions, and biases. Think of perceived credibility like a universal resume. It ultimately determines whether or not you are going to get an interview.
- *Achieved credibility* is the credibility you gain or lose based on the impression you make during interactions. If *perceived credibility* is your resume, then *achieved credibility* is how you interview. Conventional wisdom suggests that you never get a second chance to make a first impression. *Achieved credibility*

is that impression and all of the things that contribute to it, such as appearance, communication, empathy, level of expertise, and confidence level. It ultimately determines whether a prospect takes action—or, in simpler terms, how likely you are to get the job.

Breaking credibility into two distinct parts makes it a little easier to comprehend, but don't underestimate just how interconnected they are. Think of it from a dating perspective. You ask a buddy to set you up with their attractive acquaintance. If that acquaintance doesn't know you or doesn't know you well—or maybe even if they do—you can almost bet they're going to google you and peruse your social footprint to figure out if they are interested enough to say yes. Do you have some likable pictures on Facebook? Did the newspaper interview you last fall about that charity you're involved with? Or, were you recently acting like a jerk to strangers on Twitter? (Of course, you weren't!) Your buddy's referral combined with what the acquaintance finds online is your perceived credibility. This is what lands you the date. Social media has all but eliminated the possibility of a real blind date anymore.

Achieved credibility, however, is based on what actually happens on the date. This is your charm, your charisma, and your connection. You keep up a great, witty conversation, and you remember to listen as much as you talk. You mind your manners. You give compliments, but only the ones you really mean. Impressing them is what lands you a second date and, eventually, a change in relationship status. Without one type of credibility, the other will be of little use. Each plays an equally important role in your success in getting past the Reflexive No. Lighthouse businesses who are honest about who they are from the get-go ensure that when their perceived credibility gets them in the door, their achieved credibility will create raving fans and loyalists. This approach is the practical antidote to over-promising and under-delivering—just deliver on your promise. This genuine philosophy can even be woven into your sales vernacular—what you see is what you get. Where others simply promise, we will actually deliver.

ENGINEERING THE OPERATING SYSTEM— DECISIONS, MESSAGING, FOCUS

To operationalize the concept of using your mission as the "true north" to guide the way you do business, challenge yourself and the people around you with the question, "Do we live what we believe?" Don't stop asking the question until you've had hordes of people from all nooks and crannies weigh in on the answer.

Dig deeper to examine how and why your organization makes decisions. Do you make them in connection with the mission of the organization or for self-preservation? Are there untouchables or sacred cows in the company that make people pucker up or shy away from promoting truth? These are tumors that blot the light out of any mission. Truth and courage are the two ingredients that create psychological safety within organizations, and it's this safety that underwrites authenticity—which, of course, is the ability to freely live out what the organization believes.

When you take a deeper look into what you believe and when and how you do or don't act on it, you need to understand what gets in the way of people working with purpose and living out the mission. If you are just starting out, think of this in the future tense: what could potentially get in the way? This could be anything from a crappy staffing model where people are chronically under-resourced and are forced to take short-cuts, to red-tape and silos. It could also be mixed messaging from leadership—for example, leaders can say that an organization prizes innovation, while in practice it suffocates it by exalting tradition and legacy.

Mixed messages are almost always delivered subtly to the recipients and are nearly invisible to those offering them. If you are a leader and you really want to know if you are perpetuating mixed messages, then you have to create a safe environment for people to speak their minds. Keep asking questions, and more importantly, listen intently to the answer without getting defensive.

Understand, likewise, that you can't get the best out of your infrastructure and talent if your company is in a constant state of upheaval. Each time there is a re-organization, priority shift, or any number of other reactive behaviors, it sends shockwaves through the masses. It shatters the belief in the organizational mission and the collective confidence in leadership's ability to execute the plan. When strategy changes need to take place, there must be transparency, explanation, and the shared ownership of failure from the top down. It is not enough to announce "the model is broken" to justify major changes that are designed to buy yourself more time to figure it out—because you never will. Instead, leadership must turn the mirror on themselves and realize that they have been asleep at the wheel for "the lost decade." They have failed to execute as much or more than those who look to them for leadership. Only after taking this ownership do they have an opportunity to communicate the course correction and regain the confidence of their team. No one expects leaders to be mistake-free. However, increasingly, there is an expectation for them to take responsibility. Tugboats never do. Life offers plenty of destabilizing change for most people, and the last thing your team needs at work is a nonstop churn of radical change activity in response to quarterly numbers, new management methodologies, or straight-up boredom at the top.

Of course, some change is necessary and good to keep things fresh. One of the key elements of a Lighthouse organization is its cultural commitment to experimentation. However, these experiments need to be undertaken strategically, purposefully, and within the overall context of advancing the mission.

An effective example is a digital marketing team that commits to proactive A/B testing of their collateral for effectiveness. If along the way, response to a campaign has been lower than expected, they don't usually lay off their staff and reallocate budget toward blimps or billboards. They would presumably collect data, learn from what works, and intentionally try new approaches that might better connect with customers. However, if your business is rolling out significant changes on a regular basis without clarity and context for your people, you simply have to understand that it's destroying the confidence of your most valuable asset. So, for your sake and theirs, cut it out. Make a plan, stick to it, and place a stated moratorium on megawatt change to give the organization enough time to make a run at it.

BOTTOM LINE

Lighthouse organizations and those who lead them leverage their mission as the central organizing principle behind how they operate. Their practical commitment to the mission as the "true north" serves to advance its brightness both internally and externally as it guides each level of decision-making. This enables the organizations to keep their credibility intact while delivering on their promises to all stakeholders. The role of the leader is to serve as a stabilizing force who exhibits patience, confidence, and intestinal fortitude in the face of adversity. They must remain attentive at all times, making subtle changes and course corrections through experimentation to avoid seismic shifts that shake the foundation upon which the collective belief rests.

REFLECT QUESTIONS

1. Think about your level of commitment to the mission of your organization. To what extent are you willing to let that mission be the "true north" to guide the decisions that you and others make?
2. Take a moment to consider the strength of your achieved credibility. Would others say that there is consistency between the image you project and what it's actually like to do business with you?
3. In hindsight, was there an opportunity where you could have taken ownership where failing to do so resulted in a heavy price? If so, what would you have done differently?

CHAPTER 9

OCCUPY MARS

My first visit to SpaceX was exactly as I imagined it would be, but better, because I saw firsthand what it looks like when an organization actually has the full weight of its talent working to advance the mission.

When I arrived, I entered a stark waiting room appointed with modern furniture, polished concrete floors, and a giant reception desk with an almost compulsory orchid at the far end. The woman behind the desk was stunning and slightly aloof behind her black-rimmed glasses. I signed in on an iPad and, after being verified, was handed a security pass that required accompaniment. The woman at the desk invited me to have a seat on the red leather chairs at the far end of the vacuous space. The anticipation made my heart flutter with excitement, like a kid going to Disneyland for the first time.

As I waited for my escort, I took in a beehive of activity while my stereotypes of rocket scientists were completely blown out of the water. Instead of nerdy pimple-faced introverts, I saw a team of young, attractive, flip-flop wearing millennials clad in shirts that read "Occupy Mars." They were visibly excited and moving in and out of the various catacombs with purpose and intensity. The energy was palpable.

After a very productive meeting about the company's growth plan and objectives, which resulted in me securing them as a client, my contact in human resources offered me a tour of the brand-new facility in Hawthorne, California. As we passed under the Google-esque staircase and life-size replicas of Iron Man, I asked about the "Occupy Mars" T-shirts everyone seemed to be wearing.

My guide nonchalantly explained, "It's the sole reason that SpaceX exists. Elon (referring to CEO Elon Musk) believes that being bi-planetary is the only way for the human race to survive an extinction event. And it will happen in our lifetime." The essence of this statement was bigger than anything I had ever imagined. It was far more significant than JFK's reason to go to the moon: "Because it's there." Suddenly, it all made sense.

As we walked through the vast hanger where parts were being 3D-printed while milled rockets were being assembled, the buzz I noticed in the lobby was amplified. It was like having an all-access, backstage pass at NASA. I was mesmerized by the grandeur of it all as much as the mission. As we walked past the cafeteria, where the day's offering was a five-dollar prime rib, everything came to a halt. In a glass room adjacent to the cafeteria was a wall that stretched from floor to ceiling, clad with monitors of various sizes. Images of a rocket being tested in Brownsville, Texas, were streaming alongside a countdown clock. I was standing in Mission Control with an anticipation that cannot be adequately explained.

The sheer size of the crowd that engulfed us only magnified the excitement. Interns, administrators, engineers, and rocket scientists all waited with bated breath. I can only imagine their emotions at the culmination of the many one-hundred-plus-hour work weeks that led up to this moment.

And then: 10, 9, 8, 7... 3, 2, 1.

On that day, the new rocket failed. There were no sighs. No tears. No sense of defeat. In spite of the day's lackluster results, the SpaceX mission had not changed, nor had the personal commitment of each individual in that room to ensure inevitable success. This unanimous dedication to the mission of Occupy Mars affords CEO Elon Musk the benefit of a highly engaged team willing to work excruciatingly long hours, make huge sacrifices, and push themselves toward a better work product. In return, the employees get to be part of something special. In fact, one employee in particular summed up this sentiment extraordinarily well in a June 2017 interview in *Forbes*:

> While no one will be forcing you to, you'll end up working crazy long hours just to keep up with your workload, and because you don't want to leave the place. A phrase I've heard thrown around SpaceX frequently is everyone is their own slave-driver. I was frequently there late at night for my job, and I never really felt alone. The factory is always alive and cranking out rockets no matter what time of day or night you go there.[7]

Mission matters to talent. All one has to do is watch the SpaceX internship trailer to get a sense of the organizational DNA and the attraction power of its mission. Everyone knows why they are there. They share a sense of purpose, mutual interests, values, principles, and an odd obsession with Legos.

Just as the brightness of a Lighthouse mission has the potential to attract consumers who are searching for it, as well as those who happen upon it by accident, it also serves to attract talented individuals who are seeking to

---

7   "What Is It like to Work at SpaceX?" Quora. https://www.quora.com/
What-is-it-like-to-work-at-SpaceX.

use their skills and abilities to further a purpose-driven organization. Lighthouse organizations set high expectations centered around the overall vision for the company, and they're sure to explain the importance of the role that talent plays in making that a reality. Lighthouses are intentional about this, because they know that it's impossible for a business to become a Lighthouse until its employees play a prominent role in the brilliance of its light.

ARTIFICIAL VS. ORGANIC ENGAGEMENT

To prove the link between mission and talent, look no further than any one of the many tools and questionnaires used globally by companies to measure what is often regarded as the number one key performance indicator (KPI) of talent development—employee engagement. A casual review of topics contained in these instruments will include questions like, "How well do you believe your work is aligned to the mission and purpose of the company?" Or, "Over the last twelve months, how many opportunities have you had to grow professionally?"

The behavioral scientists who have defined the core elements of employee engagement clearly recognize that mission and professional growth are important predictors of employee and workplace performance. And yet, it isn't uncommon for CEOs to lament about people not knowing how their companies make money, or managers not understanding the strategic fundamentals of why the business pursues a certain market segment over others. When this happens, it is not an acumen problem; it's a failure to properly harness and deploy the full power of the mission to ignite the passion and productivity of the organization's talent pool.

However, when a Lighthouse organization gets the mission/talent formula right, as in the example of SpaceX, the mission not only serves as a magnet that initially draws in talent, its strength continues to organically create engagement over the long term. The challenge is to free ourselves and our businesses from the Tugboat grind of turnover and artificially manufactured employee engagement. This is your chance to move from fits and starts to bring it all into alignment, to become that rare Lighthouse organization that finally gets this talent thing right.

BOTTOM LINE

The Lighthouse mission not only attracts talent to your business, but when properly harnessed and deployed, that same mission activates the full power and potential of the team. This alignment creates organic engagement and longevity, because people are motivated to generously lend their skills and abilities to advance the organization's mission.

REFLECT

1. Think about the current state of your talent as a whole or by individual groups. Would you describe the collective "mood" as energizing, draining, or neutral?

2. Consider the potential outcomes from having a tightly aligned mission/talent equation. What is one practical step you can take to strengthen the equation within your organization?

3. What is your company's (team's) Lighthouse mission—the rallying cry that serves to unify, mobilize, and attract talent?

PART 3

LIGHTHOUSE
TALENT

CHAPTER 10

AN ODE TO FREDO

Of the key components that set a Lighthouse business apart from its Tugboat neighbors, perhaps no element determines success more than culture. Though most ideas we've discussed—from mission to authenticity—end up contributing to culture, the topic deserves specific focus as it pertains to the role of the leader, who is not only responsible for establishing the vision and mission but also for creating an environment in which it can become a reality.

In the second film of *The Godfather* series, fans are treated to more backstory and delicious exploits of the Corleone crime family, its associates, and its adversaries. The movie zig-zags its way through family origins, a high-stakes Senate hearing, and an attempted assassination, eventually setting up a raw scene between brothers Michael (Al Pacino) and Fredo (John Cazale).

Spoiler alert: tensions are boiling hot as Fredo discloses his involvement in a series of meetings and actions that seemed innocent enough at the time but clearly were out-of-step with the best interests of the family. These would soon prove to be fatal. Calm and composed in his fact finding, Michael drives Fredo to further declare his prime motivation for this perceived treachery: "He said there was something in it for me!"

Sensing deep disapproval, Fredo continues his descent by revealing example after example of trivial tasks that he was often dispatched to undertake and his obvious conclusion that he had been stepped over and disrespected.

Though our ode to Fredo may be little more than an excuse for the gratuitous usage of *The Godfather* (if you were writing a book, wouldn't you?), there is something inherently important within it. Fredo feels like a useless cog in the system, who in turn unwittingly sabotages the interests of the organization through his actions. As the choice "opportunities and projects" were given out to those at the top of the hierarchy, Fredo grew tired of the grind. As a result, the longstanding expectations of allegiance began to wear thin. Soon, the character started thinking about what was best for him, and over time, those actions unwittingly sabotaged the interests of the family. Exacerbated by the unexpressed inner turmoil of being an outsider inside his own organization, when he's confronted the best Fredo could muster up was how he really felt.

MISSION VS. ME

In the absence of a grand mission that draws people together toward something bigger than themselves, people will naturally default to self-interest and self-preservation. The compounding effects of this phenomenon will degenerate quickly into an "every man for himself" environment, leading to the demise of even the best-laid plans.

This reality is a covert and silent organizational killer. People don't announce that they feel aimless, undervalued, confused, or disinterested. Instead they go about their days simply feigning interest, smiles, and high levels of productivity, all the while seeking purpose and pursuing self-interest wherever they can find it. The fact is that Tugboat, me-driven cultures are not only problematic, but they exist at epidemic levels. The result is a disconnected workforce in which growth is stunted, creativity is diminished, and productivity slows until eventually the entire operation is destabilized.

It certainly doesn't have to be this way. However, the cultural gardens in most organizations are left woefully unattended.

When those atop the food chain operate in a me-centric way, others notice and begin to follow suit, simply living what they've learned. Leaders look through the lens of "How do I benefit? How can I further line my pockets? What will I look like to the board or our stakeholders if we do or don't do this?" Soon others adopt this line of thinking and follow suit. The fact is that we won't get what we want—we get a combination of who we are and what we are willing to tolerate.

CULTURE DOESN'T JUST HAPPEN

Lighthouse organizations get the crux of the culture formula right by operationalizing their missions. The first step is to make the core values of the business actionable. Just by the virtue of not being saddled down by the weight of "every man for himself," makes a Lighthouse business feel, well, lighter—like a breath of fresh air. Lighthouses understand that culture isn't about abundant snacks, flowing kombucha, or ping-pong tables. It is about behaviors that align to the mission and the experiences that deepen each team member's connection and commitment to the organization. The rest of that stuff is just a nice perk.

Getting the formula around employee experience right starts from the moment an organization defines (or redefines) its core principles. Lighthouse organizations think holistically, imagining what the ideal employee experience is, then continually look for ways to exemplify what they believe at each stage of an employee's journey, making milestones within the employee lifecycle tangible and experiential. They start with a well-defined framework that can be scaled across the organization as it grows without losing the intimacy that makes startups so special.

Lighthouse organizations that claim to be family friendly need to do more than the annual family fun day or take your kids to work day. They need to be considerate and flexible. They must consider allowing their people the latitude to never miss a class trip or sporting event and encourage them to go. Perhaps they could highlight achievements through a family newsletter, offer scholarships, sponsor sports teams, have a family camping trip, or maybe just provide a voucher for UberEats, Postmates, or other food-delivery service to send dinner home when the employee has a deadline to meet that keeps them working late.

Likewise, if your mantra is "making a difference in the community," you should probably forego the all-inclusive drunk-fest at a Mexican resort for top performers, replacing it instead with building a school in Guatemala. Instead of a happy hour, volunteer at a food bank. Instead of a co-ed softball league, join your local Habitat for Humanity. The caveat, though, is that these things need to be authentic to the voice and values of your organization, so people genuinely buy in to the ideas.

In the end, the core question is whether the organization is living its stated purpose and beliefs each and every day. To that end, are the employees' experiences aligned with what they were promised during the interview? Ultimately, this level of intentional and intelligent institutional design will ensure that a Lighthouse business operationalizes its belief system into the DNA of the employee pool. This becomes the differentiator that is ultimately magnified by all of the stakeholders drawing more like-minded talent, further perpetuating the culture and mission.

FAIRWEATHER CULTURE

Lighthouses sustain a commitment to culture no matter the conditions or circumstances, because a strong culture isn't optional. The people who work for them simply must be able to count on culture remaining consistent through each of the four seasons of business—from the dawning of spring possibilities, to the afterglow of summer success, to the transitional nature of fall and, of course, the cold winds of winter.

Lighthouses recognize that people can't thrive in a yo-yo

environment that reacts to changing weather patterns. When sales are up, in most companies, that energy and optimism lead to happier people, more projects getting funded, hiring approvals for additional team members, and so on. But when sales go down, the mood instantly shifts, and panic sets in. Leaders quickly abandon their plans, hunker down, and focus on survival. Employees really struggle with seasonal cultures. While they put on a brave face at meetings, back at their desks, they are fretting about job security and the relevance of their current work, while worrying about how they are going to absorb more of the load. The "me" cycle continues to perpetuate itself.

Reactive cultures make people miserable, and those miserable people will take it out on you when responding to your engagement surveys. They may also vent on social media, or, worse, sites like Indeed and Glassdoor. These exasperated folks will tell their family and friends that working at your company is fine for now, but they have their eyes open for something better. This does not advance your interest or set your business up for success. For organizations with larger workforces, when this sentiment is multiplied across your many teams, departments, and functions, the potential fallout to your employer brand is utterly devastating. Engagement scores are lagging indicators; by the time red flags show up on employee-engagement surveys and leadership gets its aggregate report, it is nearly too late to resuscitate.

Lighthouses, on the other hand, don't let the impending fog of uncertainty, frigid winters, or other garden-variety speed bumps dictate their investments in culture. It's simply too important to the mission. In fact, as temperatures begin to drop, Lighthouses often double down on culture, knowing that it is the one thing that will help them pull through.

BOTTOM LINE

"Culture eats strategy for lunch" is a well-known business expression commonly ascribed to management guru Peter Drucker. Most business leaders will nod their heads enthusiastically in agreement over its sentiment. Lighthouse leaders understand that nurturing your culture protects both your strategy and performance. It may be the difference-maker when all else goes wrong. They don't leave it up to their people to figure out what the "words on the wall" mean. Instead, strong leaders define and model what a mission-driven culture looks like. They live it each and every day using their words and, more importantly, their deeds to operationalize the organization's core values and inspire others to perpetuate similar behaviors. The end result is the magnification of the brightness of the mission both internally and externally.

REFLECT

1. How do you translate your core values into everyday actions and behaviors that advance the brightness of your mission?

2. What are some ways you can monitor the environment to ensure that you are contributing to a culture of "we" instead of a culture of "me"?

CHAPTER 11

THE YANKEES WAY

There are many things that I am thankful for when it comes to my parents. They instilled in me an indomitable work ethic, a sense of self-determination, and the freedom to make decisions (even risky ones) as long as I was willing to accept responsibility for the outcomes. There's no question that I would not be the business leader I am today if not for their support and role modeling. That said, they are not without flaw.

You need not look any further than the fact that, though raised in the New York Metropolitan Area where better options abounded, I was brought up to root for the New York Jets, Knicks, Rangers, and Mets. Some would say tongue-in-cheek that such suffering can only be attributed to well-intentioned, though nonetheless bad, parenting.

As you can imagine, I faced taunting and ridicule from friends, relatives, and complete strangers about my fandom—all of which was tolerable. I could easily laugh at opposing fans who reminded me that Mets actually stands for Mildly Entertaining Through September or embrace the replays of the now-infamous Mark Sanchez butt fumble. However, what is completely intolerable are the cross-town rivals who always seem to win. There is nothing worse than the self-loathing and angst that comes every time the Canyon of Champions plays host to another New York City ticker-tape parade celebrating a NY Giants Superbowl victory—four of which have occurred in my lifetime ('87, '91, '08, and '12). Let's not forget the New York Yankees World Series victories that seem to nauseatingly repeat almost every October ('77, '78, '96, '98, '99, '00, and '09). It is in these moments that I am reminded how joy has been stolen away from me. One World Championship for the Mets (1986) and one Stanley Cup for the Rangers (1994). Zero for the Jets or Knicks. Some say that the misery is what being a real fan is about. I submit that I would trade an entire life of sports misery and the glimmer of hope that springs eternal through my utterances of "wait 'til next year," if I could have just turned back the hands of time and been born a New York Yankees fan.

There are few, if any, sports franchises that embody what it means to be a Lighthouse more than the New York

Yankees. With 100 percent certainty, I could use their club as a model to speak to any of the attributes we have discussed to this point. We could talk about culture, differentiation, a willingness to experiment, prioritization, or the role of candor and transparency as deployed by legendary owner George Steinbrenner. The New York Yankees understand that the organization with the best players wins. They have long made the case for relentlessly pursuing and upgrading their talent, especially when they lacked what they needed internally to reach their goal—another championship.

I am certain that small-market sports fans are already dismissing this idea outright. They are quick to attribute the Yankees' success to their ability to outspend everyone else, and they would be justified in their assessment. However, if that were all it was, the Mets would be equally loathed instead of laughed at, because no amount of spending seems to deliver anything short of consistently horrible. The difference is that the Yankees' willingness to pay big salaries comes from a core belief that doing so puts them in the best position to win. Paying a premium outweighs the risk of saving money by placing an average player in a key position.

But it's more than just a combination of payroll and the potential endorsement opportunities of a major market. The Yankees have a recipe for recruiting talent. They leverage the allure of donning the timeless navy pin-stripe uniform and combine it with the majesty of walking upon the hallowed ground of Yankee Stadium (even the new one). They offer newcomers an invitation to a fraternity and the potential to have a place in Monument Park alongside Mantle, Marris, DiMaggio, Ruth, Gehrig, Stengel, Jackson, Rivera, Pettite, Posada, and Jeter. Since the days of Murderer's Row, the Yankees have come to understand that talent begets talent, and stars attract other stars. When they get the equation and chemistry right (which they have more than any other team in history), the individual's contribution is magnified and the aggregate performance is accelerated. The result is a franchise synonymous with success that attracts the best of the best in droves—especially those in search of an elusive World Series ring and a chance to be a Yankee.

FALLACY AND FRUSTRATION

As a candidate, I have only gone on five interviews in my entire life. Two were for restaurant jobs in my teens. Two were for internships—one of which led to my career path. And one was to take a corporate Vice President position for a Fortune 200 company. But I've been on the other side—the hiring side—of the equation for thousands of them. Those collective experiences left me with one resoundingly decisive opinion. *I hate interviewing!*

Painful amounts of posturing make almost every interview nearly unbearable. Often recruiters and human resources professionals sit in judgment across the table, asking a bunch of ridiculous questions like, "So what are your strengths and weaknesses?" and "Where do you see yourself in five years?" These same interviewers misrepresent their value proposition as one that is aspirational and fulfilling, when really, they just need to fill a slot on an organizational chart. Instead of sharing their authentic selves, candidates are forced to audition so that they can "win" the job. Self-important executives and misrepresentation by candidates are the makings of a bad relationship right from the get-go. It's not unlike dating, where once the glossy veneer someone put on to impress someone else dissipates and their true qualities show through, both are parties unhappy, feeling like they've wasted the last six months of their lives. Never in the hiring process should anyone sit in judgment, but rather, they should seek to discover what makes the person across the table tick.

The main objective of any interview should be to discover reasons why someone might or might not be successful or a good fit within your open role and, more importantly, within your culture. To do so, it is important to identify a certain set of decision criteria beyond just being "attracted" to them. In business, just as in sports, the relative bargaining power of top talent is immense. If you don't realize upfront that the power has shifted toward them, you won't win many recruiting battles. As much as you are interviewing them, they are interviewing you. To attract the very best, you need to institute a recruiting approach where you identify and then meet each of the factors that cause the top players to accept a position. It's equally important for you and your hiring team to stop acting arrogantly, as if you possess all of the power in the hiring relationship. At least for talent that is in high demand, you need to realize that the candidate is the one who holds most of the power. This requires corporations to develop a more candidate-friendly recruiting experience that seeks as its first objective to identify completely a candidate's job acceptance criteria.

Our recommendation is to be candid with them from the outset and see how they respond. Not only does this establish your business as one that believes in candor and honesty, but it also makes you more aspirational. Stop looking only for quality candidates, and start searching for candidates with the qualities that you seek—those who are drawn to your mission, who are worth your investment and developmental attention. Be transparent about what you believe will make them successful, and only extend to them the hand of opportunity if they have the potential to be the superstars your team deserves. Step out from behind your desk. Sitting behind it is the ultimate assertion of power and position—not a way to invite someone in. As noted above, seek to understand what is important to the person you're speaking with. Listen intently to each of their answers, and probe beyond the surface level bullshit answers. Find out what research they have done on the company before your conversation. Ask them what they saw within that research that piqued their interest enough for them to pursue an opportunity with you. Ask how they think their time at your company will help them on their journey in life. Candidates' answers to questions like these are as important as their technical skills and abilities to perform the function that you need. All of this information, once secured, will be the basis upon which you either sell them on joining your mission or eliminate their candidacy.

RELENTLESSLY PURSUE UPGRADING YOUR TALENT

The way that job seekers—your potential talent—are engaging with the employment market is remarkably different than in decades prior. LinkedIn research demonstrates that 87 percent of all employees are actively or passively considering a job change,[8] and I'd guess that the other 13 percent are probably those who own the businesses or government workers who intentionally chose

---

8   *The Ultimate List of Hiring Statistics For Hiring Managers, HR Professionals, and Recruiters.* LinkedIN. Accessed December 21, 2018. https://business.linkedin.com/content/dam/business/talent-solutions/global/en_us/c/pdfs/Ultimate-List-of-Hiring-Stats-v02.04.pdf

a path with the least amount of interviewing and performance demands. But that 87 percent is a staggering number. It speaks to the fact that people are in a continuous state of openness to new opportunities. Talent becomes an impulse buyer who will leave their current role for what they believe is a bigger, better deal. This continuous state of openness is a tapestry where the threads of discontent loom and grow. Sources of this discontent may range from less-than-ideal working conditions, to compensation models that are not aligned with individuals' perceived value, or it may crop up after a consecutive series of particularly frustrating days. Moreover, they might just be looking for a new relationship of value to replace the one that has lost its luster.

With the vast majority of the workforce looking all the time, the emerging gig economy provides an enticing alternative for those who are particularly entrepreneurial and talented and offers them a way to regain control of their destiny. Of course, this new crop of self-empowered talent joins the rest of their currently-employed-but-always-window-shopping counterparts, which makes it even harder for businesses to use outdated hiring methods and still function. The status quo of hiring really hasn't changed much over the last twenty years. Classified "Help Wanted" ads have been replaced by their digital equivalents of Indeed or a company careers page. While applicant-tracking systems have eliminated the need to mail in hard-copy resumes, after prospective talent sends in their applications, they're still left in the dark. Whether or not it's an external recruiter or an internal hiring manager who perpetuates these actions is irrelevant, because the outcomes are the same. The approach isn't meant to "recruit" talent, in the genuine sense of the word, but simply to hire them into existing roles. Hiring is an inefficient, transactional process that simply doesn't align with the attitude, timing, or expectations of modern talent.

TALENT AGGREGATE

Lighthouses don't just hunt for talent as they need it—they make its identification an apex priority and are unwavering in their commitment to farm it over time. They prioritize their most important positions. Lighthouses recruit strong individual contributors and those who understand the value of being part of a team. Now does this sound familiar compared to your recruiting organization? Do you have a brand name that packs clout? Do you have the resources to close the deal when needed for candidates? Do you have a reputation for driving forward employee's careers? If this sounds like your organization, then great.

The next step is just finding the talent you want and using your weight and resources to get them to join your company. While you'll lose a few, in the end you'll get more than your fair share that you target.

If you're not the Yankees, then you need to get more creative. Possessing this type of focus is what allows you to capitalize on the ebbs and flows of the human capital pool and ratchet up your talent aggregate.

The talent aggregate is a composite score that indicates the current team's ability to advance the organization's mission. It considers individual roles, leadership capabilities, and other critical contributions. Armed with the most current talent aggregate score for their organization, Lighthouses are always on the lookout for those who can literally move the needle and strengthen the overall impact of the team. When they discover someone who can do just that, they find a way to bring them in by creating a role if one doesn't already exist.

Lighthouses hire the best talent because they have a comprehensive talent cultivation strategy. Before a business becomes a household name (or in Google's case, a verb in Webster's dictionary), where the brand itself serves as a beacon to draw the best talent., business that want the benefits of Lighthouse attraction must be intentional in their strategy. They need to engineer a magnetic field that gets and keeps the attention of top-tier prospective talent. They do so by leveraging every possible resource they have. They send out messages to the masses through social media by creating content and leverage interpersonal interactions and employee relationships to grow their reach and influence.

This is not dissimilar to how a marketing or sales team builds its pipeline. When a great prospect comes in, the team uses carefully planned touchpoints to capture and cultivate that prospect. As time goes by, this subtle yet proactive approach builds valuable connection.

After people become aware of a Lighthouse business, that business's talent cultivation strategy may expand to include more focused touchpoints, like extending open-house invitations for future talent to interact with current team members and see the Lighthouse culture on full display. The strategy might include a newsletter that highlights the success, growth, and cultural goings-on in the company. More importantly, your recruiting strategy should include content specifically designed to provide value to prospective talent. You might offer complimentary professional development resources or mastermind classes. The goal is to get candidates to begin imagining themselves inside a world with extraordinary employer commitment to their success. It is likely they will begin to envy those lucky enough to be on the inside. You might also invite them to company outings such as a night at the local minor league baseball game, a ping-pong tournament, or your community philanthropic endeavors. Create an exclusive Facebook group, or send a personal *handwritten* note. The goal of all of this effort is that when their thread of discontent grows, and the timing is right for a change, your business is the first place they think of. Most importantly, never give up. Just because they may spend a long time in the prospective cultivation system does not mean they are any less valuable to helping you reach your goals. The average employee in the United States changes jobs every 4.4 years—so it's just a matter of timing.

DIVERSITY AS A STRATEGY

L'chaim Foods is a catering company based in San Francisco that produces personal and professional events for the Who's Who of the Bay Area. What makes this operation especially interesting isn't necessarily its thought leadership around the future of artisan kosher cuisine, or even that revenues have grown by nearly 50 percent over the last year.[9] Well, maybe the double-digit growth is interesting, but what's more interesting is the *why* behind it. Proprietor Alex Shandrovsky has a very unique talent acquisition strategy. He works with local prison-reform organizations to hire ex-cons, with a

---

9   Shah, Kinjal Dagli. "Why This Small Business Owner Only Hires Ex-Felons." Gusto. September 19, 2018. Accessed December 21, 2018. https://gusto.com/framework/business-secrets/lchaim-foods/.

preference for lifers—the longer the prison sentence the better. He knows that longer sentences often correlate to the complexity of the offense, increasing the likelihood that prospective candidates ran enterprises—albeit illegal ones—that involved managing people, supply chains, and similar levels of business involvement. Shandrovsky, an immigrant, believes that this population of ex-cons display many of the same qualities that made him successful, including a desire to be part of a community and a vision for only one possible outcome—success. He isn't cavalier in these pursuits and has a well-defined approach for sourcing, onboarding, and incentivizing his new hires. He's built a team where his Executive Chef, Sous Chef, and Director of Operations are all former inmates, each on a path to becoming a full-fledged partner in the operation. As a small business, being able to tap into an unconventional candidate pool with transferable skills gives L'chaim Foods an advantage. Giving these unconventional and often-overlooked individuals the opportunity to be leaders and owners creates an incomparable work ethic, while the tax breaks are the glaze atop the apple cake. The fact that L'chaim Foods turns the typical recruiting paradigm on its head is one of many interesting aspects about this story. Of course, not everyone has to embrace this particular model, but Lighthouses must look at the potential talent pool with fresh eyes and be strategic about attracting diverse individuals who want to advance the organization's mission.

Talent diversity is a most worthy pursuit, but it needs to be more than a corporate doctrine. It can't be about quota or bragging rights. If leadership is asking itself, "Who do we have to hire to win this type of recognition or to get our CEO on the cover of that magazine?" then they are missing the point entirely. We promised candor upfront, and while we recognize the taboo nature of this next statement, we're going to be blunt anyway: when companies hire and promote someone whom the average person within the organization would say isn't quite ripe for the role, just to fulfill diversity requirements, this move immediately weakens the company's credibility and quietly calls into question leadership's motives and overall judgment. Diversity for the sake of checking the box does no one any favors and offers zero value.

Lighthouses recognize that they are better off when their workforce mirrors the marketplace that they want to serve. When considering the talent options that they have to take on, the first consideration always goes to shared values, commitment to the mission, and the mix of transferable skills. All things being equal, Lighthouse businesses eagerly pursue diversity as a strategy, because they believe that with diversity comes perspective. These organizations know that genuine diversity is more than just another way to get your name highlighted in a magazine. It enhances their organization's ability to amplify the mission and serve the market.

BOTTOM LINE

The thread of discontent and new opportunities means that talent is in a continual state of readiness to leave their current roles for what they perceive to be a better deal. Lighthouses are continuously looking to add new talent and deploy a talent cultivation strategy to ensure they attract the best and the brightest to their team. They also genuinely believe in diversity and seek to build an eclectic team of people who believe in the mission while reflecting the marketplace they serve.

REFLECT

1. How can your business capitalize on the growing threads of discontent among the broader workforce?
2. In what ways can your team engage with prospective talent as part of a talent cultivation strategy?
3. What steps can you take to pursue genuine diversity as a strategy instead of just "checking the box?"

CHAPTER 12

TALENT DESTINATION

When the average US couple celebrates the start of their life together, they spend approximately $35,000 for the wedding event. If you talk to a couple who has been married for more than thirty years, though, they will probably tell you that, sure, they admire all the fun and fanfare of weddings, but the real celebration isn't just one day of extravagant fun. The real celebration is in the day-to-day, honoring the years of commitment and sacrifice to one another.

Businesses spend extravagantly too. When the average US company calculates the expense of interviewing, hiring, training, lost productivity, and opportunity costs to replace a mid-level position, it amounts to more than $120,000 per person, far higher than your average wedding. Consider the impact if a business experiences 20–40 percent (or higher) workforce annual attrition—that is, people leaving and needing to be replaced. The turnover equation is a serious, destabilizing force that people too often accept as normal. Now factor in the changing talent attitudes and expectations of the prospective workforce we discussed in the last chapter, and you can see that stubbornly sticking to the status quo will only make your business more vulnerable to employee discontent, and therefore more vulnerable to attrition, too.

Even though they are aware that the forever employee is akin to a unicorn, Lighthouse businesses are serious about keeping their promises to their talent and are willing to put their time and money where their mouths are. As part of the business strategy, they craft a talent value proposition that is both authentic to them and meets the needs of those who work for them. This approach requires some agility, so while the business will build the framework and determine how much it will invest, it's the talent that shapes both offerings and experience. A strong talent value proposition framework likely includes robust professional development, guided philanthropy, dynamic working environments, and lifestyle enhancements.

ROBUST PROFESSIONAL DEVELOPMENT

The days of hiring in mass, dropping them in a class, and giving them a swift kick in the ass are over. So too is throwing a bunch of poorly designed, nonsensical materials on a learning management system for self-study. Lighthouse businesses understand they must do more. They understand that while providing a digital "hub" of content is still an acceptable utility, modern professional development is experiential and is driven by the interests of the learner. They combine access to video-based, masterclass content, then sponsor a lunch where people can come together and discuss ways to apply the lessons. They create a peer-to-peer environment where people can post new ideas and share discoveries for others to try. There are no freeloaders and no non-participants. From the CEO on down, all are encouraged to engage and matched accordingly.

Traditional mentorship is replaced with structured meet-ups where people can proactively engage with others in the organization who have a certain area of knowledge and expertise. In this model, the authority can provide specific coaching or guidance to solve a problem or simply arrange a professional introduction to someone else. There should be guided learning and your own version of Google's "dog food," where people are free to experiment and socialize about what they have found. The goal is always to invest in people by developing them for the short-term while preparing them for whatever their future holds. Consider gamifying professional development and adding a contest element to increase engagement. The more people that tap into the offerings, the more they are recognized and rewarded. A learning organization is an improving organization—stick with it, even if it takes a while to gain traction.

COMPANY MBA

On August 16, 2018, NYU announced that all 442 students who were attending their School of Medicine would be able to do so free of having to pay tuition ever again. The goal of this action, according to Chairman of the Board Kenneth Langone, was to provide graduates the ability to "walk out of here unencumbered, looking at a future where they can do what their passion tells them." In a press release, NYU explained that this was the culmination of an eleven-year plan to encourage diversity, help the best and brightest that could not afford medical school, and solve for underserved specialties that doctors could not afford to pursue because of debt. With this act, NYU not only amplified its status as one of the nation's top medical schools, it became a mission-driven Lighthouse attracting the best and brightest talent—all but guaranteeing that they will have their pick of the litter to fill each one of their 442 medical school slots. They will have this competitive advantage and all that comes with it (at least until Harvard, Johns Hopkins, or UPenn decides to follow suit).

In the 1970s and 1980s, listing Xerox sales training

on your resume was all a hiring manager needed to see before making the candidate the VP of Sales offer. Through their commitment to differentiation by active selection of the right candidates, an investment in training, and robust coaching, Xerox became synonymous with sales. They became a Lighthouse, attracting all who wanted to glean value from their experience on their way to becoming sales savants.

More recently, Enterprise Rent-A-Car has made a huge splash among new college graduates by creating a hands-on management training program focused on application of theoretical skills learned in school. Without this commitment to training, they would be hard pressed to attract talent into positions that might appear to be little more than a glorified carwash attendant. Enterprise understands that their commitment to and investment in their people delivers results, including a J.D. Power Award for "Highest in Rental Car Customer Satisfaction" for the fourth consecutive year. They understand that employees who are attracted by their value proposition of professional development will soldier through an untold amount of unspectacular work for the payoff of an elevated pedigree.

There is a preponderance of evidence that suggests that companies are starting to take notice and move beyond perks and ping-pong tables to attract the talent they need to survive. Many are doing so with gritted teeth, wondering if the return on investment will be there, considering employee tenure is on the decline. There is perhaps no better exemplification of this idea than in the form of a cartoon that surfaced on the internet, where a CFO posits, "What happens if we invest in developing our staff, and then they leave?" The CEO smartly responds, "What happens if we don't, and they stay?" The fact is that companies that want to compete are left with no choice.

Investing in development of your people with "a grain of salt" is the wrong attitude if you want to establish yourself as a Lighthouse that attracts talent. Instead you make it the central priority of your employee value proposition.

A while ago, I had the opportunity to meet and listen to a man who has been at the top of his field in the world of food for decades, Thomas Keller. The only thing more difficult than getting a table at his Napa Valley mainstay known as The French Laundry is getting your foot in the door for an apprenticeship. During his talk, Chef Keller said, "Teach your team to be better than you. Once you've trained them, it's mutually beneficial to maintain a mentor relationship with them. You never want to take their training away. There are always new things you can teach them. Their achievements become your successes." This philosophy has led to a prolific list of a modern who's who of chefs—the likes of Grant Achatz, Rene Redzepi, and Ryan Poli. Keller's fingerprints on these standouts ensure that there is no shortage of applicants willing to start out washing dishes for the opportunity to learn from this culinary master.

Increasingly, Americans are questioning the value of college education, especially when it comes with a price tag and a mountain of debt well into six figures. Likewise, many companies have started to assess whether checking the college degree box is all that necessary. This was highlighted in an October 8, 2018, story conducted by CNBC that identified twelve brands that no longer require a degree as a prerequisite. You might be surprised that Google, Apple, IBM, and Hilton are all on the list.[10] These companies value experience, demonstrable skills, and a commitment to personal growth over a four-year liberal arts degree in underwater basket-weaving.

Thanks to readily accessible, low-cost technology, there is a real opportunity for companies large and small to step up and be a disruptive force in today's educational climate. Whether they build it internally or partner with content providers, Lighthouses have the potential of disintermediating higher academia as we know it. To do so they will have to broaden their instruction, offering

10   Connley, Courtney. "Google, Apple and 12 Other Companies That No Longer Require a College Degree." CNBC. October 08, 2018. Accessed December 21, 2018. https://www.cnbc.com/2018/08/16/15-companies-that-no-longer-require-employees-to-have-a-college-degree.html.

a slate of topics beyond a myopic masterclass in product, process, or "the company way." They will need to move beyond the compulsory "sexual harassment" and "anti-money laundering" required course load to create comprehensive college-like curriculum that is interesting, is engaging, and brings real developmental value to the student/employee. If they do so successfully, it may lead to a reality in which eight years of experience in Hilton's developmental program starting out as a front desk receptionist becomes every bit as respectable as, and perhaps more valuable than, obtaining a master's degree in Management and Hospitality from Cornell.

Deploying this strategy, along with a commitment to Thomas Keller-like mentorship and coaching will give those that deploy it a major recruiting advantage in the marketplace to continuously siphon the best talent. It will likewise ensure that the arduous process of today's succession planning is replaced with a continuous stream of highly-skilled and culturally-adept talent ready to step in when the opportunity presents itself as a result of healthy turnover.

GUIDED PHILANTHROPY

Philanthropic acuity creates a triple win for Lighthouses. Beyond the obvious benefit to those on the receiving end, Nielsen research has shown that 66 percent of respondents say they're willing to pay more for products and services that come from companies who are committed to positive social and environmental impact, up from 55 percent in 2014 and 50 percent in 2013.[11] Even though the research is a few years old, this quantitative discovery supports observable cultural shifts where people desire to be part of something bigger than themselves—and it isn't slowing down. When philanthropy within an organization evolves beyond the token golf outing for charity or a dinner and silent auction and is consciously woven into organizational life, it begins to align with these shifting cultural values. It isn't long before actual profits follow suit.

Even more, a commitment to social impact through guided philanthropy is an engagement accelerant for talent. When a Lighthouse makes space in the day to do good for others and organizes experiences for their people to give back, it creates deep centers of gratitude in both the employee who is performing acts of service and the community benefiting from them. In both cases the emotional halo strengthens the collective bonds that both groups have with the organization. Philanthropic efforts that are integrated into the way that Lighthouses do business tap into a deeper level of humanity and become a major differentiating factor in the talent value proposition.

---

11   The Sustainability Imperative, 2015.

DYNAMIC WORKING ENVIRONMENTS

While not every business has a large budget to design office spaces that are on par with the startup charm of San Jose's Silicon Valley (or Santa Monica's Silicon Beach!), there's always an opportunity to synchronize the environment with the needs of your talent. In doing so, people feel inspired and at ease to do their best work. Instead of thinking about cubes or a "bullpen," think about zones. Work with your team to co-design multiple areas throughout your space where people can have meetings, collaborate, decompress, innovate, learn, and do quiet work. Provide coffee makers and snacks throughout. Surprise people by bringing in goodies and wheeling around snack carts. Sign up for leadership conference live streams, pipe them into your conference room, and encourage people to stay awhile.

Beyond office configurations, consider how the work gets done within the environment. Engage your talent in creating a living document that describes the top ten mission-based principles that govern the way people think, talk, and act about the work they do. For example, one principle could be, "Candor unlocks clarity." The accompanying definition would serve to help leaders to strive for transparency, individuals to communicate with directness, and groups to use candor as a tool to drive progress. Post these principles throughout the space, add them to the top of internal meeting agendas, and continually recognize when people use them in their everyday work.

LIFESTYLE ENHANCEMENTS

Lifestyle enhancements are not to be confused with mere perks. They are curated and offered to talent because they serve to make people's lives easier and more enjoyable. As an example, consider how personalized health assistants could help employees navigate the time-consuming and often frustrating health insurance landscape. Consider facilitating a personal concierge, onsite dry cleaning, or yoga. You don't need to pay for it—just make it easier. Your people will appreciate partnerships that create efficiency and lower the cost, so obtain agreements with national and local providers that entitle them to preferred service and discounts on things like: pet sitting, childcare, computers, entertainment, fitness, auto-repair, and groceries.

Deploying a thoughtful strategy that helps people live better lives actually solves for the work-life-balance jargon that's easy to say but can feel impossible to do. When Lighthouses integrate lifestyle realities into workplace offerings, it adds a welcomed dimension to its talent value proposition.

TURNOVER ISN'T EVIL

Though the opening paragraphs of this chapter spoke to the costs of turnover and the need to stave it off, the fact is that trying to do so is an exercise in futility. The career life cycle of our grandparents is out. No longer is it normal for an individual to spend forty years with one company working their way up the career ladder, stopping at each wrung, until they retire with a pension just in time to augment it with Social Security. That model of yester-year has been replaced with something that more likely resembles a career lattice—full of experiential moves where candidates pick up skills or just want a change of scenery and a new challenge. Some of these moves are leaps forward, and some are more lateral in nature, but they are always predicated on the candidate's perception of value and experience.

A finely tuned talent value proposition enables people to have those experiences from within your organization. When the time comes that someone has exhausted the resources and utility your business has to offer, they will likely choose to move on. However, that sort of turn-over isn't evil. Those who leave a Lighthouse after years of being developed and equipped do so with a tremen-dous amount of gratitude. They are also highly likely to find someone else with high potential and refer them to the business, wanting that person to reap the same benefits they did during their time there. This is a far different scenario than the kind of turnover that happens prematurely because people are dissatisfied, and it's far less costly.

Lighthouses embody a sincere belief that their people are the most important part of their business. This is why they are radical about creating the right combination of environment and experiences to bring their mission to life and enable their talent to thrive. Consider again the SpaceX example; as the team stood by waiting for the rocket to launch the buzz coming out of that factory was palpable. It was an indicator that a little piece of them was so deeply connected to the success of the mission, there was no earthly (or marsly) way they would miss being there until the end. All the snazzy career websites in the world don't hold a candle to someone enthusiastically declaring just how much they love what they do, where they do it, and who they do it with. In most cases, it's not rocket science.

BOTTOM LINE

Just like the marketplace has changed, so too has the vertical career paradigm. Longevity with a single company has been replaced by a more modern, agile career where people make experiential moves to pick up skills or seek out new surroundings while they embrace their next challenge. Understanding this new normal is your first step to crafting a strategy that will help you capitalize by becoming a destination for those in transit, and it is a mechanism that will help you keep people as long as the relationship is mutually beneficial, maximizing productivity. Lighthouses differentiate themselves through the value proposition they deliver to talent. They significantly invest in education, experiences, and resources that will position people to reach their next level of success. Their goal is not to make employees indentured servants, but rather to ensure that when talent ultimately does move on that they remain advocates who encourage others to work for the business. Lighthouse businesses instinctively know that measuring success based on how long people stay is no longer relevant because of employee transience. Instead they have decided to try to affect what their former employees say after they leave. They make this investment knowing that this is the ultimate amplification of mission to the market and attractor of the next generation of talent upon which they can fulfill their ultimate purpose.

REFLECT QUESTIONS

1. Think about your career up to this point. What were the top three defining experiences that elevated you to where you are today?

2. Consider one element of value that is authentic to your organization that you could offer employees as a

way to invest in them. What would it take to activate and deploy that value?

CHAPTER 13

LEADERSHIP NON-NEGOTIABLES

It's the end of a long, grueling year for a small team at a services firm who has banded together to face far more than your garden variety of challenges and setbacks. First there was something of a mass employee exodus, when three members of a fifteen-person team decided to leave in the same six-week span. Then the usual client scrambles were compounded by a full slate of internal development projects that left the skeleton crew day-lighting, moonlighting, and everything in between. At a team get-together just before the holiday break, the collective exhale in the air is unmistakable. The CEO, who fancies himself to be rather in tune with people, thanks each of them for their hard and diligent work that year. He proceeds to express flowery platitudes, extolling the virtues of collaboration, determination, and teamwork. To the delight of most in the room, one of the other leaders gifts each team member with an Amazon Alexa. The predictable jokes ensue. Wonder what Alexa is going to hear in *his* house and so forth. As the obligatory laughter dies down, members of the team are just about to check out of the meeting when the CEO makes a final, yet not so subtly suggestive remark. "I am sure each of you are going to enjoy some time with your family," he says. "I will be in full-on planning mode for next year and may be reaching out to some of you by email over the break, but it likely won't be urgent. Happy Holidays!" Collective inhale. Silence. *Did he really just say that?*

Bereft of emotional intelligence, that leader has no idea how that whole scenario has played out for the people in the room. After an especially challenging year, the team that was gathered for a meal just wanted to hear a "Thank you" and "Enjoy the holiday." Instead the CEO's remark sounded more like, "No rest for the weary. You guys eat, drink, and be merry, but I'll be planning for next year and won't hesitate to involve you if I need to." Those mixed messages were a total slap in the face to the staff. What they really wanted to hear was, "Enjoy your time with family, and I am planning to do the same with mine. We've all worked hard this year and earned some downtime." While some may view this leader as a driver or a pace-setter, what he really comes across as is a martyr.

This is someone who isn't just content with letting their hard work speak for itself. Instead it becomes a tool wielded to manipulate other people. To subtly remind them that their work isn't enough, because someone else is pushing harder, longer, faster. In the case of this particular CEO, the company's strategic priorities and measure of success were always shifting, and so not only did people feel like their work was often irrelevant, but they were continuously reminded through the passive-aggressive statements of its leaders that it wasn't ever enough. If you are one of those leaders prone to this behavior, stop it. No one cares about your martyrdom. Focus on inspiring people instead of guilting them.

Leaders play a significant role in not only charting a strategic course or in setting priorities, but they also set the social order in motion. They perpetuate an organization's culture through their actions and behavior. Sadly, many leaders operate in a bubble of self-importance. Years removed from the trenches, they lose connectedness with the frontline and often grow insensitive to and intolerant of difficult messaging. Watching people try to have courageous conversations with corporate windbags is painful. They perform the equivalent of speech acrobatics to make a "no" answer sound more like a maybe-possibly-we'll try.

THE LEADERSHIP DIFFERENTIATOR

There are no Lighthouses without genuine, other-centered leaders. They recognize that everything they say and do, including their omissions, are fair game. The people around them are continuously scanning those actions and inactions for meaning, continuity, and authenticity.

Leadership is critical to the life and health of the Lighthouse structure and is rooted in three main pillars: context, consistency and compassion.

CONTEXT

Tugboats are religiously shrouded in secrecy. Power typically consolidates at the top, often behind hermetically sealed doors, and others are left to scramble and grapple with incomplete tidbits of information. Speculation runs rampant. Nerves get frayed, and productivity and morale can spiral. Lighthouses, on the other hand, are led by competent and caring leaders who recognize that context changes everything. That isn't to say that nothing is off-limits in a Lighthouse organization, but its leaders recognize the wisdom in proactively sharing information with people. They share things like how the company makes money, why it's in a particular market, and what the organization's talent acquisition plans, challenges, ideas, opportunities, and shareholder expectations are, along with other things that aren't fully baked. Context is about the good news, the bad news, and, prudently, the stuff in between.

A Lighthouse leader has mastered the art and science of drawing people in while shielding only the necessities for a period of time. A commitment to providing context is a small but significant leadership tool that can pay big dividends over time. When people are informed, they feel more confident, more empowered, and more equipped to function at a high level within their role. Context also communicates that a leader trusts people to wisely use information to the fullest extent to the organization's advantage.

CONSISTENCY

The idea that Lighthouse leaders would strive for consistency is not to deny the fact that change abounds. It's quite the opposite actually. In full acknowledgement of the constant change that impacts our professional and personal lives, Lighthouse leaders have an opportunity to serve as stabilizing forces. They do this through the public control of their emotions and consistency of their own actions in spite of changing conditions. Circumstances, whether positive or negative, have no impact on a Lighthouse leader's choice to live out the core values of the organization each day. They are unapologetically optimistic and a light source unto themselves.

Lighthouse leaders understand that they are always under the microscope. They realize that while they inhabit their role, they are subjected to tremendous scrutiny, and so their words must align with their actions. They appreciate that integrity means that they have to do what they say they are going to do without exception, even when it's inconvenient. And they know what the ultimate duty of a leader is—to assign all of the success to others and all of the failure to themselves.

The opposite can be seen among Tugboat captains. It is not uncommon for these individuals' actions to misalign with their words. They are quick to utter statements like "nothing happens until a sale is made," and then blame sales for becoming lazy, overpaid, and ineffective. Failing to meet projections to investors or the Board of Directors is usually met with misdirection, the casting of aspersions, or scapegoating instead of owning the fact that they were asleep at the helm or lost in their own narcissism.

Leaders are the cultural purveyors of the organization, and to whom much is given and much is required. The difference between a Tugboat leader and a Lighthouse leader is that the Tugboat leader thinks the (cultural) rules don't apply to them and that their words alone are enough. The Lighthouse leader, on the other hand, assumes the responsibility for modeling what the culture looks like, especially when it's the harder thing to do. They look at the failures of the team as theirs to solve. Did we innovate enough? Invest in the right tools and resources? Respond properly to the marketplace? Make bad decisions, or worse—no decisions?

COMPASSION

Whoever said, "It's not personal; it's business," was surely a Tugboat ticket holder. Until robots take over the world, business is inherently about people. There is a reason why the concept of servant leadership has made its way into the leadership field of study over the last ten years. If you aspire to be a leader who truly connects not only to the minds but to the hearts of your people, then at some level you must be motivated by compassion.

Lighthouse leaders know that compassion isn't a feeling any more than a marriage that has reached its golden anniversary is about the level of euphoria felt during a first kiss. Just as in personal relationships that are built to last a lifetime, compassion in a professional setting is about commitment—commitment to the mission and commitment to your people, both your loyal consumers and, most importantly, your talent. Compassion expressed as commitment means that Lighthouse leaders follow through on promises. They keep promises to develop and to come alongside and help individuals recognize their paths forward, both at the organization and when it's time to move on. It's about seeking to understand what motivates people and why. Compassion goes beyond just saying, "Thank you for doing a great job." It lingers a while longer to specify details about how that individual furthered the mission of the company. Compassion goes beyond the ordinary office pleasantries and makes people feel valued and special. It's a mindset, a set of intentional actions, and a commitment.

BOTTOM LINE

Genuine Lighthouse leaders are a vital part of the DNA equation in that they define the culture through actions and behaviors. Lighthouse leaders operate with context, consistency, and compassion as they take responsibility for executing on the organization's value proposition to its talent.

REFLECT QUESTIONS

1. When you consider the three important pillars of Lighthouse leadership—context, consistency, and compassion—where is your greatest opportunity to focus?
2. In reviewing the list of universal needs of employees, which represent the best opportunity for you to meet that need and bring value to your people?
3. Who was the best leader you ever worked with? Why?

4. Who was the worst leader you ever worked for? Why?

PART 4

MAGNIFYING
THE MISSION

CHAPTER 14

MISSION IS THE NEW BRAND

Charity Water's website is bold in their mission that they believe they can "solve the water crisis in our lifetime." Nike believes that "if you have a body, then you are an athlete" and focuses on products for every such athlete in the world. Toms believes in a "one for one" message that every child should have a good pair of shoes. WeWork is inspired by the idea of helping people "make a life, not just a living." On a more relatable note, there's a plumber in Los Angeles called Mike Diamond. Locals will recognize him as the "Smell Good Plumber." Mike's passion is to make plumbing a less shitty experience (pun intended). There's a movement happening around us. For-profit companies are adopting nonprofit-like purpose and authentically connecting their business strategies to their mission.

BRAND EVOLUTION

Brand still helps businesses become recognizable. Humankind has long rallied around images and symbols as one of several ways we recognize and connect with messages or ideas. During the earliest generations of our ancestors, these pictures were quite literally inscribed in stone in the bedrock of their communities, on the walls of their caves. While we have continued to evolve as a species and grow in intelligence, we've retained our affinity for visuals and have even expanded their utility to serve our interests. Consider the practice of cattle branding. Dating back to the 1500s, it was common for a rancher to develop a unique mark and burn the shape onto the animal to indicate ownership or belonging.

Fast forward to the late 1800s and early 1900s, when factories gave rise to increased product output, and businesses were once again attaching images to their work. In May 1884, the oldest US trademark still in use today—SAMSON which features a design of a man and a lion—was registered for use on cords, line, and rope. More early trademark adopters included Nabisco's Cream of Wheat, Carnation brand condensed milk, and Pabst Milwaukee Blue Ribbon beer. Millions of others followed over the next hundred years.

In the late '90s and early 2000s, with a proliferation of logos in the marketplace, focus shifted from the product to the brand. Those who once referred to themselves as marketers were now brand strategists aiming to elevate the logo beyond its mere utility as a tool for consumer recognition. Now, branding was about engineering how you wanted people to *feel* about your business. For some it was about being trustworthy. For others it was about the pinnacle of luxury or the permission to indulge. Branding was the prevailing strategy that determined all types of business decisions and dominated internal conversations.

In the race for brand superiority, companies grew rabid about protecting their brands, and this worked, for a while. Enter social media, where the consumer's voice was gaining parity with an organization with a multimillion-dollar branding and advertising budget. If someone's experience was at odds with the carefully constructed image of The Brand, they now had several platforms on which to air their grievances. Or their disinterest. With a few clicks, these same consumers have the opportunity to turn down the chatter as they become absorbed with the people and conversation topics that actually matter to them. Just like that, the power dynamic shifted.

MISSION IS SATIATING

Branding is still a thing, but it's not the most important thing. In the last three years, there's been an awakening of sorts. We've all felt it. A collective distrust of anything that feels like the establishment and big corporations. Unsurprisingly, some of the world's most iconic logos fit right into the category of "big corporations." While those logos still serve in their trusty utility of brand recognition, the artificial engineering just doesn't work with consumers like it did ten years ago. People are quick to recognize when things are too choreographed, and it evokes the Reflexive No. Consider the recent backlash against airbrushing images. For a century, it was all about glossy images, until people woke up to the consequences of continuously comparing themselves to a fallacy. Recent campaigns by Dove and Abercrombie, among others, have showcased the beauty in everyday people and created some positive buzz.

What people are craving is real. They are looking for ways to connect with others through shared values and experiences. We've focused quite a bit on the importance of the mission and its value to employees and consumers alike. However, for Lighthouses, the power and potential of amplifying that mission into the market becomes a major competitive advantage. There was a time when simply relying on an established brand, well-polished and recognizable, had that sample potential and those who followed the playbook were able to reap the benefits. But today, mission is the new brand—not just a logo, but a lived and visible authenticity.

BOTTOM LINE

While branding worked for many years to create consumer awareness and engineer good feelings about a company and its products, the old tactics are no longer effective. People push back on anything that feels too glossy or contrived. By contrast, Lighthouses have a unique opportunity to leverage the authenticity of their missions to forge genuine connections with people and gain longevity through relatability.

REFLECT QUESTIONS

1. Think about some of the iconic brands you admire and enjoy. How well would you say they are able to still capture and keep your attention using tried and true messaging and media?
2. If you were to move away from the old playbook and focus on mission-driven messaging, how might your business benefit from being an early adopter of this approach?

CHAPTER 15

MAKING POSITIVE IMPRINTS

I'll confess to a bit of an addiction to men's suiting and all of the accoutrements that go with it—pocket squares, cufflinks, ties, and of course, shoes. (If you follow any of my content online, you may have surmised as much.) Upscale men's fashion has been my guilty pleasure since the first time I ventured into Victor Pascal's tailor shop in Baltimore more than twenty years ago. There is much to be said about the quality and fit of custom bespoke clothing, but for me it's so much more. It's the process of choosing everything from the perfect fabric to the cut of the lapel and the angle of the pockets, from the stitching and buttons to the lining and monograms. Fine fashion isn't only for women. Like a straight razor shave with hot towels, it is a throwback to the way things used to be, an intense attention to detail that is as much art as it is utility.

Some might dismiss the idea of spending several hours and thousands of dollars on suits as indulgent and unnecessary, but I am happy to do it without hesitation or regret. As much as I am paying for a one-of-a-kind quality product, I am also paying for the experience of standing on a box and being measured. It is for these reasons that I am fairly certain that I will be the eighty-year-old grandpa who still dons a suit to go out for an early dinner on Sunday afternoon.

You might imagine that I have a similar affinity for casual clothing, but you'd be mostly wrong—until recently that is. For years, my causal clothing was a joyless afterthought purchased at discount stores like Marshalls and TJMaxx, rarely tailored to fit, and most often an amalgamation of odds and ends purchased independently with little to no thought or curation. I was often left feeling that though my closet was full of items, I had nothing to wear. That was until I reconnected with my college fraternity brother Andrew Weitz, CEO of The Weitz Effect. In his own words, Andrew "helps men who work in fields where their professional image has a direct impact on their success. Through style, we increase one's confidence, business network, personal relationships, income and career advancement." He and I actually had a conversation on the Lighthouse Podcast about looking at fashion as an investment. It's definitely worth the listen. On and off the air, we talked about this concept in relation to my non-suit wardrobe, or what Andrew refers to as "upper-casual." Andrew provides a customized experience for his clients by seeking to understand their needs before curating quality items that are regularly available, and most importantly, tailoring them to ensure the right fit. I quickly realized that my perspective needed an adjustment, and Andrew gave it to me.

Shortly after we completed the podcast, I was departing for Greece with my family to celebrate the seventieth birthdays of my mother, mother-in-law, and father-in-law. After a visit to my closet, I realized that my wardrobe was not suitable for a yacht charter to the Mediterranean. A close friend of mine recommended I visit the newly opened brick-and-mortar Trunk Club in Culver City. Before he confidently assured me, "You will love this place," I had known Trunk Club to be a web-based company that paired you with a stylist who then selected and shipped a collection of items. This concept never really appealed to me for the simple reason that I assumed that opening a box packed by a random stranger would likely leave me disappointed with the contents and too lazy to return them. When it comes to clothes, I want to touch, feel, and evaluate the product and then decide. As such, most of my online purchases are limited to shoes and accessories. Trusting that my friend wouldn't lead me astray, and knowing that he enjoys the bespoke experience as much as I do, I called his Trunk Club stylist and scheduled an appointment for that afternoon.

When I arrived, I was greeted at the front desk with a warm welcome followed by an inquiry about what stylist I was there to see. The well-dressed and attractive greeter moved swiftly into action, ushering me to one of several well-appointed personal sitting areas. She sat me on a perfectly weathered smoking chair and asked if I would like a beer, some wine, or perhaps a cup of tea, or coffee. I asked for sparkling water. "Pellegrino?" she offered, I nodded, and off she went leaving me to take in the surroundings. The exposed wood rafters and open floor plan with wide-paneled, gleaming wood floors were perfectly complemented by subtle, yet intentional touches to remind you that you are there for an experience. The space offered the warmth of natural light and aromas of coffee, leather, and the familiar smell that reminded me of Victor Pascal's tailor shop. What I didn't see were racks of clothes. Instead the interior designers opted for a menagerie of displays that served both as decoration, and a reminder that you weren't just hanging out in Restoration Hardware's Beverly Hills showroom or some hip advertising agency.

My stylist soon appeared. She made quick with the

small talk and then peppered me with a series of questions ranging from the occasion for which I was shopping to the brands and styles I've worn in the past. After taking some measurements, she disappeared into the voluminous employee-only space at the back of the store. A second stylist appeared in her absence, complimenting my custom suit and asking if I would give her a shot at winning my business. I sipped my sparkling water, refusing to commit, and we shot the breeze until the first stylist returned with handfuls of items that she'd pulled from the hidden racks. There was an ebb and flow of things I loved and things that were absolutely not my taste. She swapped out what was ill-fitting and brought new garments to replace the ones I'd dismissed outright. At times, we haggled a bit over style, but refusing my two new fashionista friends was an exercise in futility. More than once they said, "I really like that on you." It came across as sincere and authentic. This was probably the case, because they were also in sync on the other items they rejected with a hardy "no." After an hour or so, we had reached a place of content, and we conducted one final sort through what I would take and what I would not. My stylist identified a few items that required complimentary alternations and wrapped the rest into bags for transport. Out of nowhere, the greeter magically appeared again to collect my credit card for payment of the items, which had already been logged into their system. She returned moments later with a receipt with more numbers on it than I'd been expecting.

At first, I was a little taken aback. I had not once during the process looked at a price tag. And though I regularly spend three times that amount on suits, I had never before indulged within the realm of upper-casual. But the sticker-shock quickly evaporated as the satisfaction of the comprehensive experience set in. In fact, I immediately went home and began telling everyone about my experience, including my wife, who demanded her own wardrobe upgrade, too. At least we looked amazing in Greece!

RETAIL IS DYING, OR NOT

There is a common belief that brick-and-mortar retail is dying. And you only need to look at the balance sheets of retailers like Sears, Kmart, JCPenney, and Macy's to find some validation. It's true that online sales, too many malls, a shrinking middle class, and millennials who value experience over materialism have damaged many of these former industry stalwarts. Companies like Zara have figured out that their clients want the exclusivity and limited availability of high fashion brands like Prada and Gucci, but they want to pay prices more in line with The GAP. While these strategies can help retailers stay out in front, pure product-based strategies are more

Tugboat than Lighthouse in terms of longevity. The winds of change will keep blowing.

However, Lighthouse retailers are poised to thrive. Through evolution or by design, they are capitalizing by understanding what the consumer really wants. As an example, Nike has captured the imaginations of would-be shoppers by offering an opportunity to play before buying in some of their marquee locations. Other locations offer the ability to customize your favorite Nike gear from shoes to team jerseys. Perhaps the most innovative addition is the integration of the digital environment with the physical, where through their downloadable app customers are not only offered in-store exclusives, but also the opportunity to pay without having to stand in line. In the next chapter, we'll talk about how Nike embraced new media and opened its circle to include authentic messaging.

The very core of a Lighthouse business is about casting a vision so bright that it draws in people who want to be part of something special. That last part is really important as we turn our attention to amplifying your message in the marketplace. To do that well, you have to know what it is that you're selling—in other words, you must have a clear grasp on the value that compels your consumer to do business with you. Once you capture the ethos of your mission and translate that into the aforementioned value, you will be able to leverage three concepts that

Lighthouse organizations use to their distinct advantage as part of amplification: messaging, experiences, and texture.

THE ALLURE OF TEXTURE

Trunk Club is a fascinating example of what knowing why people are doing business with you looks like. Capitalizing on their stated mission to help people build better wardrobes, they know what business they are in, which is the service of making shopping easy and fun. Every message they push out builds upon this idea, but where it really comes alive is in their Clubhouses, which are situated in select US cities including Los Angeles, New York, and Chicago. The moment you are in a Trunk Club Clubhouse, you notice décor that coyly reflects the vibe of that particular city. There's also a handsome beverage bar prominently situated within the space, which beckons the consumer to have a drink first before getting down to the business of dressing. The experiential nature of Trunk Club and its Clubhouses serve up positive impressions, one atop the other, which add up to the consumer feeling that shopping is indeed easy and fun. They've done this exceptionally well because they know exactly what business they are in and the value that they bring.

You don't need the sophisticated flair of a luxury services business like Trunk Club to leverage many of the same elements to advance your own efforts. Whatever business you are in, you can choose to build an environment for the people who work for you. The type of consumers that you will attract is an important layer when differentiating your business. This is the allure of texture, which is quite simply the various elements and factors that work together to drive how people feel when they walk into your space, visit your website, or interact with your organization in some other way. Some of these factors are obvious—your logo or colors, which extend to the other design elements. However, another way to nail texture is through going hyper-local and incorporating meaningful touches from the neighborhood or region where the business sits. This can take the form of black-and-white photos of local scenery to serving coffee and other beverages from the area.

ZERO IN ON VALUE

It's not surprising that Trunk Club's parent company is Nordstrom, who bought them in 2014. Trunk Club aligns with Nordstrom's strategic priorities around superior customer service, fashion, relevance, and a seamless shopping experience. Almost everyone has heard the tale of the snow-tire wielding customer and the gracious and committed employee who without hesitation accepted the item as a return at his local Nordstrom Department Store. As the story goes, despite the store not selling tires, the employee had no choice but to accept the return due to his unwavering commitment to and appreciation of the company's core belief that "the customer is always right," and an understanding that if you exceed expectations at every opportunity, you will have "a customer for life."

Regardless of whether this story is an urban legend or a factual account, its proliferation into the consumer psyche is the byproduct of a value-obsessed and customer-driven culture. Over its nearly 120-year history, Nordstrom has evolved from a single shoe store into a retail behemoth synonymous with customer service. It was a company ahead of its time with an understanding that its products and pricing could not be the only differentiator. Nordstrom also understood, as far back as 1929, the power of social selling and its ability to magnify the brightness. A prominent sign in the store window read: "If we sell you well, tell others. If not, tell us."

The value that your organization brings to the market is going to heavily influence your messaging, and it's important to be accurate and attuned to what your value actually is—and for some people, it isn't always obvious. The first step in recognizing the value your organization brings is to ask yourself a few questions, beginning with "What triggers consumers to do business with us?" Next consider the range of emotional reactions that consumers feel when things go right and when things go wrong.

When things go wrong, why is that? What fear or frustration does that illicit on the part of the consumer? Putting the answers to these questions together serves as your GPS for nailing what consumers actually buy. In other (rhyming) words, it's why they buy.

We've talked a lot about higher-end retailers thus far, but let's look at another example. Let's say you own a tow-truck company, and consumers aren't buying your tow package. Well, sort of, but not really. Think about how someone feels when it's two o'clock in the morning, and it is dark, cold, and pouring rain. They are stuck on the side of the road with a flat tire, and your dispatcher gets the call. What this tired, soggy soul wants is safety, rescue, and reassurance. That's what you are selling. If your tow truck driver shows up with a cup of coffee and a compassionate smile, he might have made a friend for life, and your business will have made a very positive impression. Likewise, think of a real estate professional. They aren't selling houses, they're selling expertise, advocacy, and concierge-level service. There are a million real estate reps out there, all with their smiling mugs splashed across bus stop benches and paper diner placemats. However, when you want to sell your property but don't have the "cream puff" home that everyone is banging down the door to buy, you need someone who's in your corner to help you get the deal done. An expert who will advise you every step of the way and be proactive to serve your interests—that's the value being sold.

POSITIVE IMPRINTS

Once you have clarified the value you bring, you're better able to leverage texture and experiences to make positive imprints on your consumers. The concept of imprinting is an important one. When we talk about the mechanics of amplifying your message, it's about deploying a strategically blended approach of pushing out content that reaches and resonates with your consumer. This is usually a combination of digital marketing, social media, original video content, and perhaps local, community-based experiences. Each time one of these messages reaches and resonates with consumers in the market, we call this imprinting. When these people actually start to do business with you and find that those interactions are consistent with what they've come to know about your organization through your messaging, the positive imprints deepen the strong impression they have about you. The more imprints and the greater the impression, the more likely that consumers will be able to quickly recall your business when the time is right.

To be clear, what we're talking about is more than marketing. Marketing, specifically content marketing, is one important aspect of this multi-prong approach to creating awareness about your organization and its mission and amplifying the value you bring. You aren't marketing so much as you are messaging, and that's an important distinction.

Messaging is more about storytelling. The beautiful part about storytelling is that, scientifically, humans are wired to connect to stories, and they retain information conveyed through stories better than through other forms of communication. When seeking opportunities to amplify your message, a longer-form blog may be a great way to share more of a story's color and details the reader may indulge and linger over a bit longer. However, social media, which we'll cover in more depth next, might be a more snackable way for your business to tease out more of the savory highlights, enticing people to engage and share. The opportunities are evident and endless. When Lighthouse organizations commit to messaging and use the power of storytelling, it results in positive imprints upon positive imprints that create lasting impressions on consumers.

BOTTOM LINE

Lighthouse organizations know exactly what business they are in and the value they bring. By planning and deploying a multi-prong approach, especially storytelling, to amplify messaging, Lighthouses can attract those who are looking for the value you bring and those who happen upon it by chance. Each time you reach and resonate with consumers, you leave positive imprints, which makes your business memorable and subject to quicker recall in times of need.

REFLECT

1. What are you selling? A commodity? Time? An experience?
2. How can you make the customer experience one that will be repeated over and over, leading to more business? Is there a way you can better use texture to your advantage?
3. In what ways could your business be making positive imprints on people?

CHAPTER 16

GETTING SOCIAL

A Sunday morning workout at LA Sports Club led to a chance encounter with a friendly and easygoing guy who warmly introduced himself with a southern drawl, "I'm Charlie. It's nice to meet you." We shared a few comments about a news story that was playing on one of many nearby TVs before parting ways for our respective workouts. About an hour later we picked up the conversation where we had left off. Charlie shared with me that he was training to complete in an Ironman in New Zealand and that his best intentions of a big workout resulted in little more than his visit to the sauna where we now sat. We had a good laugh about intentions and the importance of showing up, even when you don't feel like it. I shared with him that this was one of the keys to my professional success. About five minutes in, it clicked. I quizzically asked, "Are you that guy whose story I saw on YouTube about losing all that weight?" I had seen his remarkable story after it had been reposted by Gary Vaynerchuck days earlier. He smiled and coyly replied "Mmhmm."

Charlie, known in the hip hop world as CEO Charlie, left Atlanta and his role as manager of 2 Chainz with a Grammy award in hand and headed for California in pursuit of starting anew. His decision not only changed his place of residence, but it would alter the trajectory of his life, helping him to get healthy, reverse a brain tumor, and transform himself from a three-hundred-plus-pound CEO to Ironman, and eventually so much more.

As Charlie shared his story with me, I was mesmerized by his passion to leverage his illness not just as a catalyst to change his life, but rather to "change the world." I instantly knew that his was a story my audience needed to hear, so I invited him to be on the Lighthouse Podcast. (Search my Soundcloud for my conversation with Charlie Jabaley to listen.) Toward the end of the podcast, Charlie exclaimed, "All it takes is one person to see or hear this, and my whole life can change." He has used this philosophy and the power of social media, building momentum toward achieving his dreams.

CHARLIE ROCKET

Needless to say, my instincts about Charlie were spot

on. A compelling mission and five powerful words at the end of a YouTube post launched Charlie Rocket, Jabaley's hero persona, into the social media stratosphere when Nike decided that his was a story worth sharing with their more than seven million Twitter followers. It may have been the boldness of instructing "Insert Nike Logo Here" on the closing black screen, but more than likely, it was the proceeding two minutes and twelve seconds of social media brilliance. A mock commercial challenged the company to stand behind their mission statement, which reads, "If you have a body, you are an athlete," while weaving together a story of professional success and physical failure, of childhood aspirations and unfulfilled dreams. It is a story of tragedy and triumph, of failure and hope. Mostly it is one that challenges each of us to consider our own limiting beliefs. If you haven't seen it already, search for "Charlie Jabaley Fan Made Nike Commercial." You will notice that it is filmed in what Jabaley refers to as his "I am you" perspective, where the viewer sees the relatable imperfections of an individual to which they otherwise attribute heroic characteristics. Charlie invites you on his journey before proclaiming, "MY STORY ISN'T OVER YET," suggesting to the viewer that neither is theirs. In doing so, he urges each viewer to reimagine their dreams and press on in making them a reality.

This action achieved its intended goal of striking nerves

within all who saw it, including those on Nike's corporate campus which was abuzz as Charlie's story permeated its walls. With their adept marketing sense, Nike saw this both as an opportunity to step up for one of their loyal stakeholders as well as a way to make a bet to capitalize on the wave of attention that Charlie was creating in his own right. In addition to the re-tweet, they invited Charlie to their facilities in Portland, where they offered him the support of their top coaches and trainers as well as piles of branded swag normally reserved for their stable of elite athletes. As he has set out to do, Charlie was officially a Nike athlete with his self-made video eclipsing more than a million views.

If the story stopped here, it would still be amazing, but it does not. At the time of this writing, Charlie's Instagram page has him in New Roads, Louisiana, more than 1,500 miles into his journey of biking across the United States. He is doing so on what he is calling "The Dream Machine Tour," traversing the country from Santa Monica, California, to Charleston, South Carolina, and eventually on to New York City. His goal is to bring attention and awareness to getting healthy because, in his words, he "had enough of the negativity and polarization [and thought] that it's time for something positive!" Along the way he is capturing the stories of others and changing lives. So far, Charlie and his team have paid off the mortgage of a teacher in California who was suffering from cancer and purchased a car for an unsuspecting Starbucks employee who had overcome abuse in a foster home, but had no way to get to back and forth from work to the University of Texas where she had earned a scholarship. Each time Charlie rolls into a new city and captures these stories on his social media platforms, his mission garners more attention. In just a single morning, he traversed the chasm from new media to old, as his story is being reported across virtually every major broadcast network—CNN, Headline News, ABC, CBS, NBC, and Fox News. Rest assured Charlie's "STORY ISN'T OVER YET." Join me in tuning in to see what's next.

Update: In the time between writing this chapter and the completion of the book, my prognostication about Charlie Jabaley has manifested itself on multiple fronts. Charlie not only finished biking across the United States, but he leveraged this achievement to garner more attention and get featured widely across mainstream media. Nike elected to include him among superstar athletes LeBron James, Serena Williams, and others in one of the most culturally relevant commercials of all time. In it, Colin Kaepernick's voiceover proclaims, "lose 120 lbs and become an Ironman—after beating a brain tumor." The award-winning and controversial commercial closes out with this assertion: "Don't ask if your dreams are crazy; ask if they're crazy enough."

Charlie's brand of craziness continues to gain momentum. He is rewriting the rules of social media. Instead of showing sunshine, rainbows, and Lamborghinis, Charlie's social media platform seeks to build deep connection through an honest dialogue with his fanbase, one where he remains vulnerable, sharing what are often raw and emotional updates. His public struggles are met with fan encouragement, and his achievements are lauded as an inspiration by his more than one hundred thousand highly-engaged Instagram followers. As a result, he has been able to launch a top-rated podcast entitled "The Charlie Rocket Show." I'm not certain what will be next for Charlie Rocket, but I encourage you to pay attention.

MAXIMUM AMPLIFICATION

When I was a neophyte entrepreneur, I was told that the way to imminent success and wealth was through hard work and cultivating the right contacts. One of my mentors advised me to always exercise the "3 x 5 rule." In simplest terms, the concept was that within three feet of wherever I stood, there was someone willing to give me five minutes of their precious time. Within that five minutes, if I could bring value, there was at least one certainty and one possibility. The certainty was that by repeatedly sharing my vision, goals, and plan, I would develop a stronger constitution, increase my overall confidence, and strengthen my resolve to persevere in the face of challenge. The possibility that existed within each of these interactions was that the person you were speaking with could change your life (sounds incredibly similar to Charlie Jabaley's comments), either in the short-term by becoming a client or in the long-term by becoming an advocate, an investor, or a source for new employees or strategic connections. Needless to say, I have told my story many times, and the results are clear—the 3 x 5 rule was a powerful tool in my success.

When it comes to a social media strategy, a similar yet even more powerful amplifier is at your disposal. According to Kit Smith at Brandwatch, as of April 2018, the total worldwide population is 7.6 billion. Of that population 55 percent use the internet, and 3.03 billon maintain social media accounts. Sprout Social suggests that within the Facebook world, everyone is only 3.5 degrees of separation away from everyone else (not the six degrees Kevin Bacon made so famous).[12] In other words, thanks to the maturation of the Internet, the smart phone, and social media platforms, you are less than four organic shares away from reaching everyone in the connected world.

These numbers may leave some salivating at the potential revenue associated with the idea of even a small fraction of these individuals converting to become clients. I would

12   "It's Actually 3.5 Degrees of Separation, Says Facebook." Fortune. Accessed December 21, 2018. http://fortune.com/2016/02/05/facebook-separation-degrees/.

offer that if this is your fixation, you are being short-sighted and missing the bigger picture. When Lighthouse businesses understand and utilize this idea correctly, their leaders can artfully advance their goals, amplifying their mission to attract both clients and talent alike.

I am certain that some cynics will suggest "nothing happens until you sell something," and I am not one to disagree with that sentiment. But in today's crowded marketplace, sustainable conversion and long-term market prowess will never occur unless you capture your prospects' imaginations and build deep connections. Lighthouse organizations amplify their messages with an intention to become part of the public consciousness, understanding that mission has either displaced entirely or at least become the core component of branding. Those who miss this key point will continue to throw good money after bad, seeing little result and nominal transaction.

This focus on amplification demands a shift in perspective and the shedding of old ways of thinking around advertising spend. It requires an understanding that your efforts are not about the short game of immediate transaction. Instead of sending your Tugboat into the harbor to collect one ship (client), you are making a commitment to shine your light (mission) into the murky darkness beyond your line of sight. In effect, you are projecting the brightness of your mission for the sake of mission itself. You're illuminating a path for those that are searching for it, and also for those who stumble upon it by mistake. The hardest part is that you must do so even when there are no ships in sight, for as long as it takes. Most people usually just give up.

This is why Charlie's "fan-made" commercial was such a powerful example. It was intentionally designed to build deep connection and bring value to his organic audience while artfully attempting to grab the attention of an influencer—in this case, Nike—who could accelerate his message to the broader marketplace. Charlie had no immediate goal of a monetary transaction, yet he has crept his way into the national spotlight, earning millions in free advertising for his mission in the process.

VIRAL-ISH

So, can anyone with a clever campaign "go viral?" Unfortunately, it's not that easy unless you capture "the Evolution of Dance," your kids being hilariously doped up on pain meds after oral surgery, or how really cute your pet hedgehog is—oh wait, those have already been done.

The fact is that very few campaigns spread like wildfire from person to person to person like a flu epidemic. In fact, a majority of your posts will only be seen by your organic network of loyal followers, with only a small percentage being shared beyond one degree of separation. (Facebook's new algorithm almost guarantees it on their platform.)

However, with the right intention and a well-thought-out strategy, you can increase your chances of exploding like a contagion, and it doesn't take getting noticed or shared by influencers like Selena Gomez, Christian Renaldo, and The Rock, or companies like Red Bull, Apple, or Nike—though that would be an amazing result, too.

Here are some things to consider:

1. Create content that moves and motivates people to engage and share. Humans are emotional beings that love stories—particularly ones that they personally identify with. Remember Charlie's "I am you" philosophy as you try to connect.
2. Be authentic! Speak directly to your audience and don't worry about those with whom your message does not resonate. The world is a big place, full of different personality types. When you know who you really are and project that to the world, you will be amazed at what happens.
3. Mix it up. While always remaining steadfastly focused on bringing value, don't be afraid to provide your audience a smorgasbord of different content that touches

different nerves. The same goes for the time of day. It's true that we love consistency, but we also crave variety. Think about a restaurant that only served one food item or never bothered to change its menu or offer specials. Even if you loved the restaurant initially, at some point you would likely get bored. The same holds true with content consumption. Content consumers want to be inspired. They want to laugh. They want to learn. Most of all they want variety. If you always drone on about the same thing, your audience will look elsewhere to satiate their appetite for variety.

4. Aesthetics and sound quality are almost as important as the message. Thanks to the volume of content being produced, there is an increasing expectation that the quality of your content pleases the eyes, the ears, and the brain. Though the occasional in-car live stream is worth part of a diverse strategy, you need to be more than a one-trick pony if you want to maintain the audience's attention.

5. Keep it tight. My rule of thumb is that if the viewers' legs would fall asleep while they were sitting on the toilet, then your content is too long. The exception to this is keynote addresses and podcasts, which have high engagement thanks to car rides and the user's ability to play them in the background or listen to them in piecemeal. Other than this, though, get to your point quickly.

6. Leverage your network of friends, fans, advocates, and employees by asking them to share often. You may even want to incentivize such behaviors with rewards. This is increasingly important, because some platforms, like Facebook, prioritize content from friends and family over businesses. Getting friends, fans, advocates, and employees to repost not only helps you beat the algorithms, but it also lends instant credibility, since a repost is often viewed as an endorsement and an organic share generates sixteen times the engagement of a sponsored or paid post.

7. What works today may not be optimal tomorrow. Strategies have expiration dates. Presumably, posting first thing in the morning, in the mid-afternoon, and in the early evenings would show the highest engagement rates because people check their social media accounts when they wake up, again when they get to work, after lunch, and then again after dinner. As a general rule of thumb, this may be true, but each platform is measurably different, and they all have their sweet spots. Tools like SOCI, Inc., and Hootsuite can help you manage campaigns and leverage key metrics for optimization. For those on a budget, you might simply search "best times to post on social media" and then experiment.

8. Monitor the results, focusing on engagement (not followers) with the biggest objective being shares (where applicable), as they multiply your reach and increase likelihood of being consumed.

9. Expect the trolls—there will always be unhappy souls that feel the need to speak negatively—but ignore them.

10. Engage, Engage, Engage! Ignoring your potential and current customers on Facebook can be detrimental. Try highlighting your best customers and reply to any questions that arise.

11. Be patient and stay the course. It will likely take time to build momentum.

BOTTOM LINE

A modern social content strategy builds awareness of your mission to the marketplace and helps to create meaningful connections with people. The strongest content is genuine, organic, and experiential. It offers a glimpse into what your company believes, sets larger-than-life goals, and invites people to become part of the action. Lighthouses commit to their content strategy and use insights to learn more about their audience, not to get them to buy something. Over time, this approach builds trust and relational capital, which cultivates opportunities for deeper engagement.

REFLECT QUESTIONS

1. Consider the current state of your online presence and your use of social media. Would you say that it is a strategic area of focus or more like checking a box?

2. Identify one interesting story to tell about your business. Think about the various ways you could carve up that story and share it via social media over the next two weeks to engage followers.

CHAPTER 17

SHINE ON

We've covered a lot of ground in this book, and throughout the process, we've encouraged you to consider the reflection questions at the end of each chapter. Now it is decision time. You will either put this book down and let the busyness of your present circumstances blot out the calls to action that will position you for success, or you will put pen to paper and answer the challenge to throw out the old playbook. We hope you choose the latter.

To get you started, let's summarize. We've used the illustrative metaphor of a Lighthouse for what a business or individual must be in order to reach maximum potential. Except most businesses and entrepreneurs operate like a Tugboat in a harbor. Tugboats move one ship at a time, battling against headwinds and peril. They are susceptible to the changing environment and extremely reliant on the expertise of their captains. They are limited in their capacity and unable to scale. Tugboat businesses are at the constant mercy of human failure and changes in the marketplace. Consumer and talent acquisition is costly, time-consuming, and just plain difficult—and not getting any easier.

Lighthouses, by contrast, are built to withstand environmental changes and harsh conditions. With a solid foundation and quality design, they become beacons that illuminate the way for those navigating rough waters. Lighthouse businesses are limitless in their capacity. They attract consumers and the best talent in the industry through the brightness of their missions. Their growth seems almost effortless and, perhaps most importantly, they stand out on the shoreline above all others.

Be honest with yourself: Are you a Tugboat or a Lighthouse? Don't know the answer? As it pertains to your social media strategy, have you ever uttered the words:

- "I'm not good with computers." You might be a Tugboat.
- "I'm not really into the whole social media thing." You might be a Tugboat.
- "I got rid of my Facebook account because it was a distraction." You might be a Tugboat.

More than a play on Jeff Foxworthy's "you might be a redneck" comedy routine, these statements should serve as a warning not to allow yourself to fall into the trap of embracing the familiar pain that you experience every day in your business instead of the unfamiliar pain of experimentation and doing something new that could have amazing results. Be careful not to craft a narrative that justifies your inaction, whether that pertains to social media, your digital footprint, or your presence on the internet. In doing so, you are neglecting a huge opportunity to build credibility and grow your business.

The truth is, we all have Tugboat tendencies. The stories and directives contained within these pages were designed to be provocative, a means of helping you reimagine yourself, your current or future entrepreneurial venture, or the company in which you are an intrapreneur. We have attempted to provide you with a transformation roadmap to help you address mission, value, authenticity, talent, leadership, and messaging. The following section offers an executive summary of the material in this book as well as a self-evaluation to get you started on constructing your very own lighthouse. Remember that without action and reinforcement, the information we've shared will slowly fade, so use the action plan provided to take that next step, and SHINE ON!

APPENDIX

EXECUTIVE SUMMARY—THE INTEGRATED LIGHTHOUSE OPERATION

- After years of bad business behavior and marketplace noise, consumers are fatigued and don't want to be sold. This reality has created the Reflexive No.
- As a result of the many options in the marketplace and the proliferation of information, the people who buy from you or work for you are unapologetic in their expectation that you will bring them value and operate with transparency.
- Just as we are seeing with consumers, employee attitudes have been gradually shifting as well. Modern workers view themselves as investible and prioritize organizations that will help them gain the necessary skills and experiences to propel them to the next level.

- There are two different types of businesses and individuals operating today—Lighthouses and Tugboats.
- Lighthouses:
  - Monitor what has worked and watch for declining ROI. They experiment constantly (advertising, marketing, distribution) and are fearless pioneers.
  - Encourage creativity and candor at every level and, in fact, they expect it.
  - Refuse to make excuses.
  - Remain steadfastly committed to ensuring that their brand is synonymous with value, innovation, and integrity.
  - Strive to make loyalists of all employees, even those who choose to leave.
- Tugboats:
  - Stick with what worked (advertising, marketing, distribution) and are fearful of experimentation.
  - Discourage creativity.
  - Remain romantic about the past.
  - Punish heresy or, worse, ignore it.
- Lighthouses operate from a place of abundance instead of scarcity and embrace this by embracing experimentation and innovation to stay ahead of the curve and be the ones to shape consumer and employee appetites.
- Lighthouse organizations are also authentic to the core, and from that genuine self-identity flows the missions and values that drive who they are and

serves as a refreshing alternative to weary and wary consumers.

- The mission serves as a vital foundation for the organization. Lighthouse organizations leverage their mission as the central organizing principle behind how they operate. The mission is the "true north" that guides each level of decision-making, which enables these organizations to deliver on their promises and be viewed as deeply credible. This practical commitment to the mission serves to advance the mission's brightness both internally and externally.

- The mission attracts talent to the business, and when properly harnessed and deployed, it activates the full power and potential of the team as people are motivated to generously lend their skills and abilities to advance the organization's mission.

- Lighthouse leaders work to define and model what a mission-driven culture looks like. They actively pursue diversity as a business strategy and focus on delivering as much value to their employees as they do to their consumers. These leaders operate with context, consistency, and compassion as they take responsibility for executing the organization's value proposition to its talent.

- When it comes to amplifying their message to the market, Lighthouses know exactly what business they are in and the value that they bring. They cement their perceived credibility and create positive imprints by motivating customers to leave positive reviews, piggybacking off the established reputation of others, and curating and sharing stories that bring their missions to life.

- Lighthouse organizations become early adopters of new communication modes and continue experimenting to stay at the forefront of ways that people consume new information in order to consistently extend the power and reach of their messages.

LIGHTHOUSE READINESS SELF-EVALUATION

We've prepared an assessment to help you better diagnose your own beliefs and behaviors, which will provide a glimpse into where you are on the Lighthouse continuum. Don't overthink your response. If you agree with the statement, put a 1 in the Agree box. If you disagree, put a 0 in the Disagree box.

- For entrepreneurs and business leaders, think about these statements as they relate to your typical behavior and how you operate your company.
- For intrapreneurs or employees, choose your responses within the context of how you view your current organization and the actions you tend to take within your current role.

COLUMN A	AGREE "1"	DISAGREE "0"	COLUMN B	AGREE "1"	DISAGREE "0"
I recognize that people have many options, which makes it harder to compete.			As a business or individual, I have clarity around purpose and mission.		
I believe that many methods that have always worked, no matter how comfortable, aren't sustainable.			The mission serves a broader goal than simply profits or a paycheck.		
It is realistic to think that employees' expectations are evolving and that they want more from their organizations.			The mission delivers discernable value to both external consumers and internal team members alike.		
I subscribe to the concept of abundance over scarcity and believe that the world is full of infinite potential and opportunities.			The mission is compelling enough to attract talent to the team.		
Commitment to experimentation and innovation isn't a luxury; it is a necessity to obtain and maintain a professional advantage.			The mission guides all manner of decision-making, when it is convenient and especially when it is not.		
COLUMN A: TOTAL POINTS			COLUMN B: TOTAL POINTS		

COLUMN C	AGREE "1"	DISAGREE "0"	COLUMN D	AGREE "1"	DISAGREE "0"
The prevailing culture is we-centric and supports people in doing their best work.			It is easy to identify and describe the texture of our business.		
When the going gets tough, we buckle up and stay the course rather than upending our stated strategies and approaches.			A blended mix of social media and other innovative platforms (i.e. podcasting) are fully leveraged as communication channels.		
Diversity is a defined business strategy as opposed to a reactive phenomenon or a check-the-box exercise.			A significant way we generate awareness of the value we bring is through storytelling.		
Leaders generally model openness and authenticity by leading with context, consistency, and clarity.			There is an intentional effort to pull reviews and feedback from stakeholders as a way to gain credibility.		
It is a regular practice to assess and address employee needs to ensure the integrity of our talent value proposition.			As another layer to messaging, we seek partnerships with others who have strong reputations and gain exposure to their audiences.		
COLUMN C: TOTAL POINTS			**COLUMN D: TOTAL POINTS**		

LIGHTHOUSE CONTINUUM

Now add up your total from all four columns and evaluate
your readiness against the following scale.

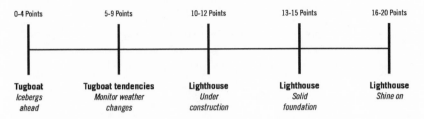

0-4 Points	5-9 Points	10-12 Points	13-15 Points	16-20 Points
Tugboat *Icebergs ahead*	**Tugboat tendencies** *Monitor weather changes*	**Lighthouse** *Under construction*	**Lighthouse** *Solid foundation*	**Lighthouse** *Shine on*

ACTION AND NEXT STEPS

IF YOU SCORED LESS THAN 3 POINTS IN COLUMN A...	Focus your attention on a change in mindset. Go back and read Part 1, Chapters 1–5.	One action that I am willing to take to activate a change in mindset over the next ten days is:
IF YOU SCORED LESS THAN 3 POINTS IN COLUMN B...	Focus your attention on mission and value. Go back and read Part 2, Chapters 6–9.	One action that I am willing to take to strengthen my mission and value proposition over the next ten days is:
IF YOU SCORED LESS THAN 3 POINTS IN COLUMN C...	Focus your attention on talent and leadership. Go back and read Part 3, Chapters 10–13.	One action that I am willing to take to deliver value to my people over the next ten days is:
IF YOU SCORED LESS THAN 3 POINTS IN COLUMN D...	Focus your attention on message and amplification. Go back and read Part 4, Chapters 14–16.	One action that I am willing to take to reach and resonate with people with my messaging over the next ten days is:

ADD YOUR VOICE TO THE LIGHTHOUSE COMMUNITY

Of course we're social. Let's talk!

- Facebook—Adam H. Michaels
- YouTube—Elevate with Adam
- Twitter—@ahmichaels
- Instagram—adamhmichaels
- Sound Cloud Podcast—The Lighthouse with Adam H. Michaels

ABOUT THE AUTHORS

ADAM H. MICHAELS is an inspirational leader and coach who is passionate about sales, entrepreneurism, and the American Dream. He has leveraged his ability to identify and develop talent to build multimillion-dollar B2B insurance agencies in several major metro markets. He has done so by cultivating a high-performance, other-centered culture where team members are bound by a commitment to personal and professional growth and a collective vision to achieve at the highest levels.

After spending much of his professional career as an entrepreneur building independent agencies, Adam joined corporate America as vice president for a Fortune 150 insurance company where he led a team of nearly 5,000 salespeople out of a decade of decline, to become an industry juggernaut with double digit sales growth and more than $256M in annual sales.

During his 25-year tenure, Adam has had the fortune of sitting across the table from thousands of entrepreneurs, CEOs, and business leaders trying to solve for the biggest issues they face in an increasingly competitive landscape. It is from these experiences and those that he had as a leader and coach that he launched his web series *Elevate with Adam*, and podcast *The Lighthouse with Adam H Michaels*, which have appreciated millions of views and higher rates of engagement than many of the most notable influencers on social media. He has been featured on Grant Cardone's *Meet the Pros* and in The Huffington Post.

DAYNA WILLIAMS has been consulting with Fortune 1000 firms on talent development and performance initiatives since 2006. Prior to that, she was a senior manager in Los Angeles, well-positioned at the critical apex of marketing and sales for a consumer goods firm. Dayna is passionate about aligning people, process, and product and has created dozens of sales, learning and culture frameworks which have been deployed within hundreds of client organizations. Her experience spans nearly the full spectrum of industries, including: Financial Services, Insurance, Technology, Hospitality, Pharmaceutical and Professional Services.

Dayna is an expert in adult learning and development. She specializes in helping organizations sustainably engage their multi-generational workforce through a blend of modern solutions. Leveraging her keen ability to identify trends and patterns that are rooted in human behavior and thus are industry agnostic, she's quick to apply lessons learned from one organization to help those across segments stay ahead of the curve.

Dayna also focuses on helping talented women reach higher levels of leadership by demonstrating how to take a strengths-based approach, combined with precise, professional development to achieve peak performance. She has served on various non-profit boards, most recently as president of the Association for Talent Development, Philadelphia. Dayna has a graduate degree in Organizational Change and frequently speaks at various conferences around the country.